THE
FOOLISH
FOUR

Foreword by
Tom Gardner

HOW TO
CRUSH
YOUR
MUTUAL FUNDS
IN 15 MINUTES
A YEAR

Published by The Motley Fool, Inc., 123 North Pitt Street,
Alexandria, Virginia, 22314, USA

Sixth Printing, November 1999
10 9 8 7 6

This publication contains the opinions and ideas of its author and is
designed to provide useful information in regard to the subject matter
covered. It is sold with the understanding that the author and publisher
are not engaged in rendering legal, financial, tax preparation or other professional services. Laws vary from state to state, and if the reader requires
expert assistance or legal advice, a competent professional should be
consulted. Readers should not rely on this (or any other) publication for
financial guidance, but should do their own homework and make their own
decisions. The author and publisher reserve the right to be stupid, wrong,
or even foolish (with a small "f"). Remember, past results are not necessar-
ily an indication of future performance.

The author and publisher specifically disclaim any responsibility for any
liability, loss or risk, personal or otherwise, which is incurred as a conse-
quence, directly or indirectly, of the use and application of any of the
contents of this book.

ISBN 1-892547-01-5

Printed in the United States of America
Set in ITC Century Book

Distributed by Publishers Group West

Design and Layout by HBP, Inc.

CONTRIBUTORS

Many wonderful Fools contributed to this book by writing, editing and updating information, researching returns, building databases, testing variations and methods, building tables and charts, and checking data. It was a lot of hard work by a dedicated team of Fools. Here are the key contributors, with our thanks:

Writing and Editing
Brian Bauer
Bob Bobala
Ann Coleman
Jeff Fischer
Tom Gardner
Roy Lewis
Selena Maranjian
Robert Price
Alex Schay
Robert Sheard
Debora Tidwell

Data / Research
Ann Coleman
Robert Price
Robert Sheard
Mona Sharma

Product Manager
Craig Fowler

TABLE OF CONTENTS

FOREWORD

The Foolish Four investment approach was developed out of the research presented by Michael O'Higgins in his fine book, *Beating the Dow*. Concentrated on enormous companies with long histories in the public markets, the investment model is the simplest and safest route to common-stock out-performance that I've ever come across. I also believe that the Foolish Four variations of the Dow Approach are a less expensive and more rewarding dish than the original recipe.

In this guide to building a Foolish Four/Dow Approach portfolio, our collection of writers has pored over the historical data, studied every angle of logic, and assembled what I consider to be the best pure-stock mechanical approach to beating the markets that exists today. Where else can you buy a handful of companies, hold them for an allotted period of time, pay long-term capital gains tax rates, and expect to have beaten the market averages in five-year bunches? With low fees, a low tax rate, and little effort, the Foolish Four and Dow Approach system of investing is flat out better than 98% of what the $5 trillion mutual-fund industry has to offer today.

Indeed, you hold a minor revolution in your hands. I hope you enjoy this guide, find it largely absent of financial jargon, and see the numerical logic behind this style of investing. As with all Fool published works, we expect to build off this effort in our online site (www.fool.com) and would appreciate any and all feedback on this guide. Please direct your comments to help@fool.com or mail them to The Motley Fool, 123 North Pitt, Fourth Floor, Alexandria, VA, 22314. As our published work extends beyond *The Motley Fool Investment Guide*, we rely on your input to guide us toward new services, new topics, and new modes of Folly.

Let's go out and beat the market.

Tom Gardner

October 7, 1998

 Keep in mind as you read this guide that, to us, "Foolish" is a positive adjective. The Motley Fool takes its name from Shakespeare. In Elizabethan drama, the Fool is usually the one who can tell the king the truth without losing his head — literally. We Fools aim to tell you truth, too — that you can beat Wall Street at its own game. To learn more about The Motley Fool, drop by our website at www.fool.com or visit us on America Online at keyword: Fool.

Part 1

MEET THE DOW DIVIDEND/ FOOLISH FOUR APPROACH

MEET THE DOW DIVIDEND/ FOOLISH FOUR APPROACH

A foolish investor (with a small "f") is one who "plays" the market, taking a flyer on some penny stocks, mortgaging his house to buy some options or futures, or trading frantically in and out of stocks by the hour. On the weekends, he checks into the local emergency room to have his ulcers treated or his heart checked. Imagine the TV drama series *Wall Street ER:*

"It's another day-trader, folks – all clear!"

(Whoomph!)

"Again. Clear!"

(Zap!)

(Lub-dub, lub-dub...)

Fear not. This book isn't about that kind of investing. Heck – that's not investing at all, really. It's speculating. Unfortunately, this is the image that many people have of the stock market – that it's a big gamble. They're wrong, though, because the stock market has a lot to offer all of us, as long as we invest Foolishly.

Foolish investors (with a capital "F") sleep *more* soundly than they did before they invested in stocks. Foolishness means learning about investing and taking control of your own finances. After all, the one who has your own best interests at heart is *you*.

We realize, though, that the average new investor isn't ready to start picking stocks on her own. That's why the Dow Dividend Approach is so perfect for beginning investors. In fact, it's such a robust and impressive way to invest that even experienced investors can (and do) benefit from it.

Let's let the facts speak for themselves. Over a period of 25 years from 1973 to 1997, the Foolish Four variation of the Dow Approach has produced an average annual return of 21.86%.

That might look good, but it doesn't really mean much without some context, so let's consider the alternatives. According to the Ibbotson & Associates *1997 Yearbook*, stocks have outperformed everything else you could have invested in during 52 out of 52 twenty-year periods since 1926. Check out these average annual returns from 1926 to 1996:

Large-company stocks	10.7%
Small-company stocks	12.6%
Long-term corporate bonds	5.6%
U.S. treasury bills	3.7%

Imagine that you invested $10,000 for a period of 25 years. If you invested the money in U.S. Treasury bills at the above annual rate of return of 3.7%, it would grow to $24,801. Not bad. Invested in long-term corporate bonds at an annual rate of 5.6%, it grows to $39,048. Better still. Plunked into stocks and growing at about 11% per year, it becomes $135,855. (An impressive difference compared with $24,801, eh?) Here's the kicker, though. If you had invested that $10,000 in the Foolish Four variation of the Dow Approach growing at 21.86%, you'd have a whopping $1.4 million after 25 years. Yowza.

Which one seems better to you? (We thought you'd say that.)

You might be worried, though, thinking that of course you prefer the higher return, but you don't want to take too much risk, and you're not sure you can master this approach. And you don't want to have to take time away from your family or your hang-gliding lessons to follow stocks. Well, we've got more good news for you. Let's address each of these concerns.

Is it risky? Investing in stocks *can* be risky. In the short-term, stocks can rise or fall without much warning. But Fools invest for the long haul, and over the long haul stocks are much less risky and have clearly outperformed bonds, gold, and Cabbage Patch collectible dolls. You just have to be strong and hold on when the market heads south for a while, which it will do on occasion. Better still, the Dow Approach won't have you investing in any obscure companies – no new-fangled MicroGenesis BioCom Enterprises here! Notice the "Dow" in the name of this approach? That means that this approach is limited to investing in the 30 companies that make up the Dow Jones Industrial Average, commonly known as "the Dow." You may have heard of some of these outfits: Sears, Wal-Mart, American Express, Boeing, Coca-Cola, Eastman Kodak, General Electric, Disney, AT&T, General Motors, IBM, McDonald's. Clearly, these are not fly-by-night operators. You can be sure they'll be around for quite a while.

Is it too difficult? When people think about investing, usually they assume that it's mysterious and complicated and not something they can master. That's understandable, given that we're rarely taught anything about investing in schools, and Wall Street types like to foster these attitudes so that people will think their money should be handed over to "professionals." The Foolish truth, though, is that you *can* master investing and you'll probably even enjoy it once you get the hang of it. The Dow Approach is just the tip of the iceberg. It's one of the first things you should learn, and it's really, really simple. Here's how simple: We tested it on a nine-year-old and he succeeded in using it to pick the correct Dow stocks. We're very sure that you can do it, too.

How much time is required? You're busy. We understand. Investing shouldn't mean that you have to give up your poker games, your Scottish cooking lessons, your daughter's track meets, or anything else. It shouldn't decrease your quality of life, but instead *improve* it. Again, the Dow Dividend is a winner. It only takes a few minutes per year. (Yup, you read that right.)

The Dow Approach has earned its place as a key investment strategy at The Motley Fool because it is one of the easiest, most time-tested, and most consistent ways ever discovered to outperform the major market averages over time. Since 1963, the average return of the each of the variations of the Dow Approach has clocked in ahead of the average return generated by the Dow Jones Industrial Average, as well as the S&P 500 index and the vast majority of mutual funds. (The S&P 500 is a popular index that tracks the 500 leading American public companies. Along with the Dow Jones Industrial Average, it's the most commonly referenced U.S. stock market index, and it's another benchmark that you, as a Fool, want to outperform.)

The table on pages 8 and 9 shows the impressive returns of several variations of the Dow Approach (we'll soon address each variation in detail) for the 35-year period from 1963 through 1997.

The logic behind the approach is fairly simple. It zeroes in on the companies in the Dow whose stocks are among the most beaten-down, pointing out which of these you should buy and hold for a specific period of time. It allows you to profit as these companies get their act together and their stock prices increase. This would be a mere theory if it hadn't been put to the test of time. We Fools and others have back-tested the approach for more than three decades. It has shown itself to be very robust and reliable, in both good markets and bad.

You may wonder where this amazing system came from. Well, it's so straightforward that establishing a single "inventor" or "discoverer" is almost impossible. The fellow who first popularized the strategy, however, is Michael O'Higgins --

who wrote the 1991 book *Beating the Dow*. A more recent effort by Harvey C. Knowles and Damon H. Petty called *The Dividend Investor* provides a more thorough analysis, but lacks the charm of O'Higgins's effort. The approach has also been covered in most major business and investing publications.

The Dow Approach has become so popular that The Motley Fool has devoted an entire online area to it, including message boards where investors can discuss the stocks, the strategy, and variations on the strategy. We even have a model portfolio showing the approach in action, complete with a nightly performance report.

But enough of this. After the performance table on the following pages, we'll get down to the nitty-gritty: How the system works. ◆

Average Annual Returns and Cumulative Total Returns

1-Year Returns (1997)	High-Yield 10	Foolish Four	RP4	S&P500	Dow 30
Average Annual Return*	20.39%	22.31%	19.49%	33.36%	22.33%
Cumulative Total Return	20.39%	22.31%	19.49%	33.36%	22.33%
$10,000 Becomes...	$12,039.00	$12,231.00	$11,949.00	$13,336.00	$12,233.00

3-Year Returns (1995–97)	High-Yield 10	Foolish Four	RP4	S&P500	Dow 30
Average Annual Return*	28.14%	25.64%	30.53%	31.15%	27.63%
Cumulative Total Return	110.40%	98.34%	122.38%	125.56%	107.88%
$10,000 Becomes...	$21,039.52	$19,834.31	$22,237.86	$22,555.86	$20,787.90

5-Year Returns (1993–97)	High-Yield 10	Foolish Four	RP4	S&P500	Dow 30
Average Annual Return*	21.63%	21.26%	25.53%	20.24%	20.52%
Cumulative Total Return	166.24%	162.17%	211.66%	151.34%	154.25%
$10,000 Becomes...	$26,623.84	$26,216.51	$31,165.64	$25,134.19	$25,425.28

10-Year Returns (1988–97)	High-Yield 10	Foolish Four	RP4	S&P500	Dow 30
Average Annual Return*	18.08%	20.91%	23.25%	18.05%	17.51%
Cumulative Total Return	426.96%	567.64%	709.11%	425.44%	401.86%
$10,000 Becomes...	$52,696.45	$66,763.75	$80,911.49	$52,543.51	$50,185.83

15-Year Returns (1983–97)	High-Yield 10	Foolish Four	RP4	S&P500	Dow 30
Average Annual Return*	19.45%	21.85%	24.86%	17.52%	18.37%
Cumulative Total Return	1,338.46%	1,837.36%	2,694.50%	1,027.07%	1,155.49%
$10,000 Becomes...	$143,846.46	$193,735.64	$279,449.93	$112,706.60	$125,548.95

Average Annual Returns and
Cumulative Total Returns cont.

20-Year Returns (1978–97)	High-Yield 10	Foolish Four	RP4	S&P500	Dow 30
Average Annual Return*	17.97%	20.76%	24.28%	16.65%	16.39%
Cumulative Total Return	2,623.92%	4,252.05%	7,622.82%	2,074.63%	1,980.25%
$10,000 Becomes…	$272,391.73	$435,205.50	$772,282.26	$217,462.73	$208,024.72

25-Year Returns (1973–97)	High-Yield 10	Foolish Four	RP4	S&P500	Dow 30
Average Annual Return*	17.69%	21.86%	24.62%	13.06%	13.83%
Cumulative Total Return	5,765.11%	13,912.27%	24,443.22%	2,052.08%	2,451.82%
$10,000 Becomes…	$586,511.33	$1,401,227.01	$2,454,322.41	$215,208.12	$255,182.44

30-Year Returns (1968–97)	High-Yield 10	Foolish Four	RP4	S&P500	Dow 30
Average Annual Return*	15.75%	19.51%	21.18%	12.12%	12.48%
Cumulative Total Return	7,818.89%	25,260.30%	30,650.40%	2,993.65%	3,309.11%
$10,000 Becomes…	$791,888.51	$2,536,029.61	$3,075,039.55	$309,364.66	$340,911.42

35-Year Returns (1963–97)	High-Yield 10	Foolish Four	RP4	S&P500	Dow 30
Average Annual Return*	15.26%	18.74%	19.84%	12.16%	12.41%
Cumulative Total Return	14,317.57%	40,671.48%	56,326.74%	5,448.61%	5,897.24%
$10,000 Becomes…	$1,441,757.29	$4,077,147.81	$5,642,674.32	$554,861.26	$599,723.63

*Average Annual Return is mathematically the same as the Compound Average Growth Rate or CAGR

Part 2

THE NUTS
AND BOLTS

THE NUTS
AND BOLTS

A lthough you only need to use one, there are many variations of the Dow Approach, several of which have been
born from the efforts of Fools tinkering together in our online
workshop. We don't want to cover every possible variation in
this book, as it's meant to be a simple introduction to a simple method. So we'll be sticking to three of the main Dow
Approach variations – the three we like the best.

The first one, which is called the High-Yield Ten, is the most
basic. Optimizing this method by testing variations yielded
our own Foolish Four and RP4 variations. This chapter
explains how to select the stocks for each approach. But first,
let's discuss what dividend yields are and why they matter.
They're at the heart of this whole approach, so it's important
to understand them before moving on.

What Are Dividend Yields?

A dividend is a payment that many public companies make to
their shareholders every three months. It's one way that a
company shares its earnings with its owners – the owners
being the shareholders. Not every company pays a dividend –
in fact, usually only established and consistently profitable
firms do. (All 30 of the Dow Jones Industrial companies currently pay a dividend.) Every three months, as they report
quarterly financial results, these firms share part of their profits by paying a fixed dividend on each share of stock out-

standing. The dividend payment is often converted in newspapers and elsewhere into a "dividend yield," so that investors can quantitatively measure in percentage terms how much an investment would yield through the cash dividend payment alone. Over the past two decades, the average Dow stock has yielded about 3% in dividend payments annually. In more recent years, the average dividend yield of a Dow stock has been slightly under 2%.

The dividend yield itself is a simple concept. Imagine that a share of stock in the New Jersey-based Hair Volumizer Co. trades for $100 and it pays a quarterly dividend of 50 cents per share of stock. That amounts to $2.00 per year (50 cents multiplied by four payments). To calculate the dividend yield, you divide the annual dividend ($2.00) by the share price ($100) and get 0.02, or 2%. Simple. With a calculator, it takes about three seconds. (Pssst… Go get your calculator, good Fool!)

Here's another, tougher, example. A share of Mr. Burrito Head Inc. trades for $43, and it pays out $1.16 per year in dividends. Try calculating its dividend yield.

(Go ahead. We'll wait.)

(The answer is coming up soon, so don't peek until you've tried the exercise.)

When you divide $1.16 by $43, you get 0.027, which is the same as 2.7%. (You can multiply the 0.027 by 100 to get the 2.7, or just remember that you move the decimal point two places to the right, as we learned in the fourth grade but often forget.)

The great thing about dividends is that unless the company is in serious trouble, you can count on getting the dividend payment year in and year out, regardless of whether the stock price is rising or falling. Even if Mr. Burrito Head's stock price remains unchanged, you still earn that 2.7% yield, which acts like an interest payment, each and every year.

The amount of a firm's dividend payment doesn't change too frequently, although several leading companies (including Dow companies) do increase their dividend payments every year because their earnings are growing every year. Not always, though. (A company in trouble might even decrease its dividend, but companies try desperately not to do that, as it scares off shareholders and signals corporate distress.)

Despite the fact that a company's dividend payment is usually a constant amount once it's set each year, the dividend *yield* does change – all the time. That's because the stock price is always changing. As the stock price rises, the dividend yield goes down, and when the stock price falls, the dividend yield rises. Consider our friend the Hair Volumizer Co. Let's see what happens to its yield (with dividends still $2.00 per year) when the stock price goes from $100 to $150 to $80 to $50. (Ouch — it's been a tough year for this company!)

Annual Dividend:	$2.00		$2.00		$2.00		$2.00	
	$\frac{\quad}{\quad}$ = 2%		$\frac{\quad}{\quad}$ = 1.33%		$\frac{\quad}{\quad}$ = 2.5%		$\frac{\quad}{\quad}$ = 4%	
Stock Price:	$100		$150		$80		$50	

See how the dividend yield rises as the stock price falls? This is the effect that the Dow Dividend Approach takes advantage of. Let's take a gander at a company like the big banking enterprise J.P. Morgan in August of 1998. It was, at that time, paying an annual dividend of $3.80. (That means $0.95 per quarter, per share.) At the beginning of August, shares of J.P. Morgan were trading at around $122 each. That's a dividend yield of 3.11%. ($3.80 divided by $122 = 0.0311) But by the end of August, the Russian economy was on the verge of collapse and the world markets, including the U.S., had taken a big spill. J.P. Morgan closed out the month of August 1998 trading at $93 per share. That gave it a dividend yield of 4.08%. As people worried about the growth prospects for this giant international banking company (which has exposure to Russia), the stock price fell. As the price fell, the dividend payment remained the same, so the dividend yield increased.

Enter the Dow Approach. It asks you to look at the basket of 30 companies that comprise the Dow Jones Industrial

Average and to zero in on those stocks with high dividend yields. Why? Because these are the companies that are likely to have seen their stock prices fall – perhaps simply because they're currently and temporarily out of favor. Since these are large, well-established companies, the system counts on most of them to turn themselves around (or, in due time, on the market simply changing its fickle mood towards the companies in question). As the companies right themselves, the stock prices will likely rise. And in the meantime, you collect a higher-than-average dividend yield.

That's the heart of the system. The Dow Approach has you buy the highest yielding Dow stocks so that (1) you collect the high dividend yield (free money, essentially!) and (2) you can also capitalize on a stock price that is likely to rise while you own it. Now let's look at the specifics of our three main Dow Approach methods.

 The Basic Dow Approach: The High-Yield Ten

The High-Yield Ten (HY10) approach (sometimes also called the "Dogs of the Dow") is the simplest and most conservative approach. It focuses on the Dow stocks with the highest dividend yields. That's it. It is that simple.

To use this method, you simply make a list of all 30 Dow stocks and calculate their dividend yields to identify the 10 stocks with the highest yields. Again, to get the dividend yield percentage, take the stock's annual dividend per share in dollars and divide it by the current price per share. (Note: Make sure dividends expressed in dollar amounts are annual amounts, not quarterly amounts.) You can get the list of the 30 Dow stocks from a newspaper like *The Wall Street Journal* or *Investor's Business Daily*, and the stock pages will also show you the quarterly dividend payment by each company. (Your local newspaper's stock listings might, as well.)

An easier way to get dividend yields, though, is to go to a source that quotes them, sparing you the calculations. For example, online you can head to The Motley Fool quote machine located on our Web site at http://quote.fool.com. If you display "Detailed" stock quotes there, you will see both the dividend yield percentage and the annual dollar amount of the dividend. Have the list of 30 Dow stocks ready (we also provide this list online at the Fool) and then enter each one and compile your list of current yields, which you'll order from highest to lowest. But wait. We saved the best for last. Online, the Fool actually provides the current list of the High-Yield Ten Dow stocks, updated every evening. (Now, that's almost making this too easy for you, isn't it? So let's imagine that we didn't just share this information.)

Because the dividend yields will fluctuate as the stock prices change during market trading, you will want to compile your list after the market closes on any particular day, just as The Motley Fool does. After that, you make your buys (as indicated on your list) at the beginning of the next business day. With the High-Yield Ten approach, once you identify the 10 stocks with the highest dividend yield percentages, you buy all 10 in equal dollar amounts. Ten percent of the money that you're investing is allocated to each stock. You then hold these stocks for at least one year and one day. (To minimize the tax bite on your returns, please see the chapter on Tax Considerations for more information on holding periods.) After the holding period ends, you refigure your list and sell the stocks that are no longer on it, and then you buy the *new* 10 Dow stocks that have the highest dividend yields. You again buy these in equal dollar amounts. Surely some of your older holdings will be on the new list, too, decreasing the amount of changes that you need to make.

Why do we reconfigure our Dow Approach holdings every year? We offer more on this topic later, but historically the back-testing shows this to work the best. After a year, typically some of last year's Dow Approach stocks have recovered in price and so their dividend yields are now lower. It serves you, then, to sell these and buy the new Dow Approach stocks that are currently sporting the highest yields. You buy the new ones, just as you did before, in equal dollar amounts. If one of your old holdings is still on the new list, you keep it, but tweak the dollar amount invested in it to make each of your holdings even again. (There is much more on this in a following section on reallocating your holdings each year.)

Note that "equal dollar amounts" means exactly that. You don't simply buy 100 shares of each stock, or 50 shares of each. You don't know which one is going to perform the best, so you want to be equally weighted in each. Not everyone knows this, but you don't have to buy stocks in "round lots" of 100 shares. Or even in round numbers like 50 or 25 shares. You really can buy 87 shares of one stock and 14 shares of another without paying any surcharges.

Let's say that you have $20,000 and you want to buy equal dollar amounts of the ten high yielding Dow stocks. Divide $20,000 by 10 and you see that you can invest $2,000 in each stock. If Stock A trades at $85 per share, you divide $2,000 by $85 to learn that you should buy 23 shares of it. ($85 x 23 = $1,955) If Stock B is trading at $32, you should buy 62 shares of it. ($32 x 62 = $1,984)

For a conservative, low-maintenance, low-stress approach, the High-Yield Ten has done very well. For the 25-year period from 1973 through 1997, the HY10 has achieved an annualized average return of 17.69%, turning an initial investment of $10,000 into $586,511. Over the same stretch, the S&P 500 has recorded an annualized return of just 13.06% per year.

What makes the HY10 approach more conservative than the variations we'll discuss next is that it has you buy ten Dow stocks, while the other variations have you invest in only four. By investing in ten, you decrease the risk that one or more of the stocks might run into trouble and have a large effect on your portfolio's performance (although you also *increase* your commission costs, because you're making six more trades). Since each stock represents only 10% of your holdings, the effect of one stock implosion will never be too great. Of course, this cuts both ways. If one of the stocks does terrifically well, it won't have as great a positive impact on your portfolio, as it initially represents only 10%, and not 25%, of your holdings.

The Foolish Four Variation

The second of the three main Dow Approach variations that we focus on in Fooldom, the Foolish Four (FF), takes the simple High-Yield Ten model one step further by re-ranking the ten stocks with a second, "low-price" screen.

While the results for the basic HY10 are impressive, they pale in comparison to the Foolish Four model. For the 25-year period from 1973 through 1997, the Foolish Four variation has returned an annualized gain of 21.86% versus 17.69% for the HY10 and 13.06% for the S&P 500. On a bottom-line basis, $10,000 invested using the Foolish Four variation starting in 1973 would have grown to more than $1.4 million by the end of 1997.

To determine the current Foolish Four stocks, you start with the High-Yield Ten list – the ten Dow stocks with the highest yields (hopefully you knew that already after reading the last section!). Look up the latest closing share price for each stock on the list. Now make a second list of these ten stocks, ranking them in ascending order by stock price per share (the lowest-priced stock in the HY10 will be No. 1 on this new list, and the highest-priced stock will be No. 10).

Compare the two lists (The HY10 ranked by dividend yield and the HY10 ranked by price). If the same stock is No. 1 on both lists, scratch it off the lists. If the No. 1 stocks are different, leave the lists as they are.

The Foolish Four stocks are simply the top four stocks on the second list (the list ranked by stock price). If you crossed out the No. 1 stock, then the Foolish Four stocks are numbers 2, 3, 4, and 5 on the list. If the top stock wasn't crossed out, then the Foolish Four are numbers 1, 2, 3, and 4. That's it.

You buy the four stocks in equal dollar amounts, just as you would with the High-Yield Ten approach. This time, though, you're allocating 25% of your money to each stock because you're only buying four. Again, hold these four stocks for at least a year and one day in order to get the long-term capital gains tax rate. When the holding period is up, you go through the calculations again to see which stocks you should be holding now. You sell what's no longer on the list and buy whatever is new to the list. (Note that during your holding period, the Foolish Four stocks on any given day might differ from the ones you're holding. That's perfectly fine and normal. The stocks in the Foolish Four change over time, and frequently. You just need to buy the ones that are correct on the day that you're buying, and then don't change them until the holding period is officially over, which is at least one year plus one day.)

One reason that this second low-price screen improves on the performance of the basic High-Yield Ten approach is that lower priced stocks tend to experience greater price volatility – that is, their stock prices will often fluctuate up and down to a greater degree than higher priced stocks. Since the assumption we're making is that the first screen (the ten highest-yielding stocks) has already identified ten good candidates for appreciation, we want to court future volatility because it's likely to be *positive* volatility. Lower priced stocks can, theoretically, more easily provide a higher percentage return with each upward movement. Focusing on four potentially more-volatile stocks out of the original ten out-of-favor high yielders tightens the model and generates better long-term returns.

If you're curious why we scratch off the number 1 stock sometimes, let us explain. It's because historical data has shown that if a stock is the highest yielding and *also* the lowest priced of the bunch (i.e., the number one stock on the second list), it may be a laggard with serious business problems, and historically it hasn't performed very well. So, we nix it, and we move to numbers 2, 3, 4, and 5 instead of numbers 1 through 4.

These four stocks are our Foolish Four stocks. You have seen the fantastic returns that they have generated in the past. If you don't wish to calculate the current stocks yourself using the method we just described, the current Foolish Four stocks are listed every day online at The Motley Fool in the "Portfolios" area. We also have a portfolio that holds only these stocks and provides a daily update – though a daily update is hardly necessary.

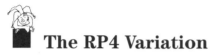

The RP4 Variation

Whereas the High-Yield Ten approach focuses strictly on the ten top-yielding Dow stocks, and the Foolish Four adds a second screen to choose four of the lowest-priced stocks from those ten, the RP ("Ratio Procedure") variation uses a single ratio incorporating both high yield and low price simultaneously. The stocks are then ranked according to this ratio. The RP is the most promising new variation of the Dow Approach that has surfaced in Fooldom. It was developed by a Fool named Bob Price. (In this book, we'll focus on the RP4 variation, which has you buy four stocks selected with the RP system. There are further variations, such as the RP2, which has you buy only two stocks. You can read more about these variations online at The Motley Fool.)

That the RP variation combines the two factors of high yield and low price simultaneously means a great deal, because the two successive screens used by the Foolish Four can sometimes lead to some illogical rankings fluctuations. For example, when a stock is No. 10 on the high-yield list and No. 2 or No. 3 on the low-price list, it's one of the favored Foolish Four stocks. The very next day the stock's price might rise just enough that it falls to No. 11 on the high-yield list, even if only by one one-hundredth of one percentage point. Poof! It's gone completely from consideration for the Foolish Four. Around the fringes, such fluctuations aren't rational, but we live with them because of the long-term success of the Foolish Four system.

The RP variation, however, combines both yield and price in a simple formula that can be applied to all 30 Dow stocks, relieving us of the artificial cut-off after identifying the top ten yielders. The formula is simple: dividend yield times dividend yield divided by stock price. It can also be represented as:

(yield x yield) / price

To make the numbers more manageable, list the yield in whole numbers rather than in its decimal equivalent. That is, instead of listing a 1.5% dividend yield as 0.015, in this formula leave it as 1.5. It doesn't affect the ratios for each stock relative to all the others and it makes the calculation easier to read.

For example, if the Free Range Onion Co. has a dividend yield of 2.76% and a stock price of $47 per share, the RP ratio for it would be:

$$\frac{2.76 \times 2.76}{47} = 0.162$$

Of the two elements, the dividend yield is more important than the low price. So by multiplying it by itself, we increase it and give it more weight.

This calculation should be done for all 30 Dow stocks. Once you're done, you rank the stocks in descending order of RP ratio. (The stock with the largest ratio is No. 1.) We run these numbers for our readers regularly and post them online for free, so to save some time, visit us at http://www.fool.com/links/currentdoworder.htm. (Yeah, that's a lot to type, but it probably beats calculating and ranking 30 ratios. This Web address is also where the current HY10 and Foolish Four stocks are listed each day.)

Once you've got your 30 stocks ranked, do you just buy the top four? No. Back-testing the model has determined that the best course is to skip the No. 1 stock. Purchase the next four in equal dollar amounts, and then hold them for at least one year and a day.

When a stock is in a bit of financial trouble, its RP ratio can be inflated (too much of a good thing). This is why the investor, more often than not, is better served by overlooking the top-ranked stock. For much the same reason, as we explained earlier, the Foolish Four approach skips the No. 1 stock in its own ranking system when that stock is both the highest yielder and the lowest priced of the bunch.

For the 25-year period from 1973 through 1997, the RP variation has generated an average annual return of 24.62%. If you recall, the Foolish Four average annual return was 21.86%, the High-Yield Ten return was 17.69%, and the S&P 500 return was 13.06% over the same period. A $10,000 investment in the RP4 beginning in 1973 would have grown to more than $2.4 million by the end of 1997.

There you have it, Fools. Three major approaches to high-yield investing in the Dow:

■ The High-Yield Ten approach, focusing on nothing but the highest dividend yields.
■ The Foolish Four, applying two separate screens to test high yield and then low price.
■ The RP variation, combining both high yield and low price in a single ratio.

All three methods point you to a group of stocks poised to perform well in the coming year. And all three have proven successful, consistently outperforming the market indices that the vast majority of professional money managers lose to year after year. Yes, it can be that easy to beat a "pro" who spent four years of college studying finance, got an MBA after that, and now spends ten hours a day fretting over the stock market. Of course, some pros are beginning to prescribe and utilize this method of investing more and more, too – so maybe you'll only tie some of them.

A Dow Approach Worksheet

As we mentioned earlier, if you come to the Motley Fool online, you'll find that each day we update our lists of which stocks constitute the main Dow Approach variations. We recommend that you take advantage of this to save time. But it's still a useful exercise to do the work yourself once, so that you see exactly how the companies are picked with these strategies. Once you understand how the simple mechanics work, you'll probably be a lot more comfortable using the system. (It's kind of like learning to do division before resorting to calculators to do it for you.) After all, what if one day you find yourself marooned on an island with nothing but some paper, a pencil, and a recent newspaper stock listing? Plus a Fool calendar and the realization that – oh no! – it's time to update your Dow Approach investments! If you know how the systems work, you can send some stock trade orders to your broker in a bottle.

Two Other Well-Known Variations

The books mentioned earlier, *Beating the Dow* by Michael O'Higgins and *The Dividend Investor* by Harvey C. Knowles and Damon H. Petty, popularized two other variations of the High-Yield Ten approach that you may have heard of – the High-Yield Five and the Dogs of the Dow Five (a.k.a. the Flying Five or Low-Price Five). We prefer the variations covered in this primer, but we thought it would be useful to cover these two briefly, since many people are familiar with them and associate them with the Dow Approach.

With the High-Yield Five approach, you take the High-Yield Ten list and buy the five highest yielding Dow stocks, ignoring all the others. With the Dogs of the Dow Five, you take the High-Yield Ten list and cull it further by selecting the five stocks on the list with the lowest share prices. You buy equal dollar amounts of each of these five stocks and hold them for at least a year and a day, just like all of the other Dow Approach variations.

So on to our little tutorial. Don't worry – you only need to do a little very basic math. And calculators are allowed. So are abacuses.

STEP 1: Following are the 30 stocks that make up the Dow Jones Industrial Average as of September 1998. (The stocks sometimes change slightly, with one dropping off and another replacing it, as we'll explain later, but this doesn't happen too frequently). In parentheses are their ticker symbols. For each of them, using either online resources or a newspaper, find out and record their dividend yield and share price.

Note: Make sure that you're recording the dividend yield, and not the amount of the dividend in dollars. The source of your information should let you know what number it's giving you. If it is the dividend yield, great – simply jot it down below. If it's the dividend dollar amount, you can easily figure out the yield by dividing the annual dividend by the share price and then multiplying the result by 100. (Example: A dividend of $3.00 and a share price of $75 represent a dividend yield of 4%. Three divided by 75 equals 0.04. Multiply that by 100 and you get 4, so it's 4%.) If you're given the actual dividend amount, and not the yield, make sure it's the amount for the whole year. If it's a quarterly dividend amount, multiply it by four to get the annual amount.

Here we go! Push back your sleeves, put your head down, and put your Foolish heart into this!

NAME OF COMPANY	Dividend Yield	Share Price
Alcoa (AA)		
AlliedSignal (ALD)		
American Express (AXP)		
AT & T (T)		
Boeing (BA)		
Caterpillar (CAT)		
Chevron (CHV)		
Citigroup (CCI)		
Coca-Cola (KO)		
Disney (DIS)		
DuPont (DD)		
Eastman Kodak (EK)		
Exxon (XON)		
General Electric (GE)		
General Motors (GM)		
Goodyear (GT)		
Hewlett-Packard (HWP)		
International Business Machines (IBM)		
International Paper (IP)		
Johnson & Johnson (JNJ)		
McDonald's (MCD)		
Merck & Co. (MRK)		
3M (MMM)		
Morgan, J.P. (JPM)		
Philip Morris (MO)		
Procter & Gamble (PG)		
Sears, Roebuck (S)		
Union Carbide (UK)		
United Technologies (UTX)		
Wal-Mart (WMT)		

STEP 2: Now, find the ten companies that have the highest yields. Jot them down below, listing them from highest yield to lowest yield. Then, list their share price. (If there's a tie between two or more companies, give preference to the company with the lowest price.)

The High-Yield Ten (10 highest yielding companies, ranked by yield)	Dividend Yield	Share Price

These ten stocks are the High-Yield Ten. That's it! To use that approach, you'd buy equal dollar amounts of these and hold them for – yes, you know – at least one year and a day. So if you have $10,000 to invest, you'd buy $1000 worth of each of the ten stocks. This might mean 26 shares of one, and 17 shares of another.

The next steps will help you pick the stocks for the Foolish Four and RP4 variations. They'll draw on the information you've already gathered above.

STEP 3: Take the ten companies above and rank them now in order of price so that the company with the lowest price is listed first and the highest-priced one is last. Enter your results below:

The High-Yield Ten (ranked by price, lowest to highest)
#1:
#2:
#3:
#4:
#5:
#6:
#7:
#8:
#9:
#10:

Note that you now have the two lists we described earlier in the Foolish Four section. The "High-Yield Ten" list is what you got in Step 2 and the "High-Yield Ten ranked by price" list is above, in Step 3.

Compare the two lists. If the same stock is No. 1 on both lists, scratch it off the lists. If the No. 1 stocks are different, leave the lists as they are.

STEP 4: The Foolish Four stocks are simply the top four stocks on the list just above. If you crossed out the No. 1 stock, then the Foolish Four are numbers 2, 3, 4, and 5. If the top stock wasn't crossed out, then the Foolish Four are numbers 1, 2, 3, and 4. Jot down the correct Foolish Four stocks in the table below:

The Foolish Four

You buy equal dollar amounts of these stocks and hold them for the correct time period before refiguring the list and switching into the new stocks. That's it!

Interested in applying the RP4 variation? Read on. We'll be building a new list for that.

STEP 5: The 30 Dow stocks are listed on the following page. You can transfer the dividend yield and share price information from the table in Step 1 into this new table. That information goes in the second and fourth columns.

In the RP variation, for each of these stocks, we'll be squaring the dividend yield (multiplying it by itself) and then dividing the result of that by the share price. Remember that you don't have to transform a 2.7% yield into 0.027. You can leave the yields looking like 2.7 and 3.3, as long as you're consistent (i.e. don't leave 1.9% as 1.9 and turn 2.5% into 0.025).

When you're done filling in columns 2, 3, 4 and 5, it's time to rank the stocks. Look at the ratios in the fifth column and assign each one a number. No. 1 goes to the highest ratio. No. 2 to the next highest. Continue until you assign a ranking of 30 to the lowest RP ratio. You should probably do this in pencil, not pen, as it's easy to overlook one item and then you'll need to revise the rankings.

Go to it, Fool! We'll meet up with you again when you're done.

NAME OF COMPANY	Dividend Yield (A)	D. Yield Squared (A x A)	Share Price (B)	RP Ratio (A x A)/B	RP Rank
Alcoa (AA)					
AlliedSignal (ALD)					
American Express (AXP)					
AT & T (T)					
Boeing (BA)					
Caterpillar (CAT)					
Chevron (CHV)					
Citigroup (CCI)					
Coca-Cola (KO)					
Disney (DIS)					
DuPont (DD)					
Eastman Kodak (EK)					
Exxon (XON)					
General Electric (GE)					
General Motors (GM)					
Goodyear (GT)					
Hewlett-Packard (HWP)					
IBM (IBM)					
International Paper (IP)					
Johnson & Johnson (JNJ)					
McDonald's (MCD)					
Merck & Co. (MRK)					
3M (MMM)					
Morgan, J.P. (JPM)					
Philip Morris (MO)					
Procter & Gamble (PG)					
Sears, Roebuck (S)					
Union Carbide (UK)					
United Technologies (UTX)					
Wal-Mart (WMT)					

STEP 6: Now, in the table above, take note of the top five stocks (those ranked 1 through 5 according to RP ratio). You'll want to disregard the No. 1 stock. In the table below, enter those ranked 2, 3, 4, and 5 from the previous table.

The RP4 stocks
#2:
#3:
#4:
#5:

You did it! These are the four stocks you'd buy if you were going to follow the RP4 variation of the Dow Approach.

You just completed the calculations to find the HY10, the Foolish Four, and the RP4 stocks – all three in one blow. (You might now be looking for a giant beanstalk to climb.) Congratulations!

Getting the Rankings and Data Online

At the Motley Fool's free Web site, we've got a lot of Dow Approach information for you, most of which is updated every day.

You'll find the main page for Dow information at http://www.fool.com/links/dowinvesting.htm. We're also on America Online, as you might already know (sorry for repeating!), at keyword: Fool.

There you can read about the approach and its variations, including any new developments. You'll also find our current rankings of Dow stocks for each of the several variations, including the High-Yield Ten, the Foolish Four, and the RP4.

Wait, there's more.

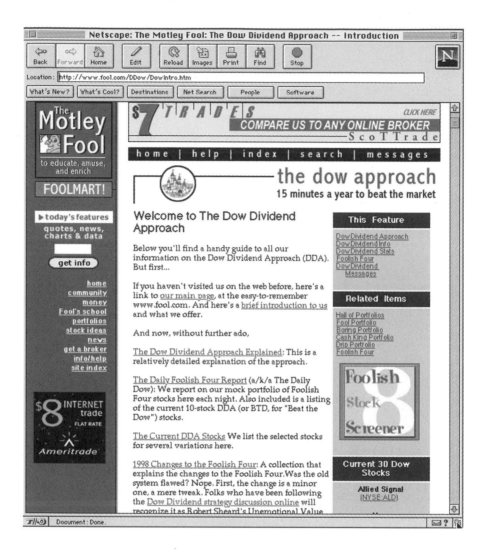

Back | Forward | Home | Edit | Reload | Images | Print | Find | Stop

Location: http://www.fool.com/DDow/DowIntro.htm

What's New? | What's Cool? | Destinations | Net Search | People | Software

The Motley Fool
to educate, amuse, and enrich

FOOLMART!

▶ today's features
quotes, news, charts & data

(get info)

home
community
money
Fool's school
portfolios
stock ideas
news
get a broker
info/help
site index

$8 INTERNET trade FLAT RATE
Ameritrade

$7 TRADES
CLICK HERE
COMPARE US TO ANY ONLINE BROKER
ScoTTrade

home | help | index | search | messages

the dow approach
15 minutes a year to beat the market

Welcome to The Dow Dividend Approach

Below you'll find a handy guide to all our information on the Dow Dividend Approach (DDA). But first...

If you haven't visited us on the web before, here's a link to our main page, at the easy-to-remember www.fool.com. And here's a brief introduction to us and what we offer.

And now, without further ado,

The Dow Dividend Approach Explained: This is a relatively detailed explanation of the approach.

The Daily Foolish Four Report (a/k/a The Daily Dow): We report on our mock portfolio of Foolish Four stocks here each night. Also included is a listing of the current 10-stock DDA (or BTD, for "Beat the Dow") stocks.

The Current DDA Stocks We list the selected stocks for several variations here.

1998 Changes to the Foolish Four: A collection that explains the changes to the Foolish Four. Was the old system flawed? Nope. First, the change is a minor one, a mere tweak. Folks who have been following the Dow Dividend strategy discussion online will recognize it as Robert Sheard's Unemotional Value

This Feature

Dow Dividend Approach
Dow Dividend Info
Dow Dividend Stats
Foolish Four
Dow Dividend Messages

Related Items

Hall of Portfolios
Fool Portfolio
Boring Portfolio
Cash King Portfolio
Drip Portfolio
Foolish Four

Foolish Stock 8 Screener

Current 30 Dow Stocks

Allied Signal
(NYSE:ALD)

Document: Done.

On our Dow Investing and Foolish Four message boards, you'll find people discussing the Dow Approach and its many variations 24 hours a day. It's a great place to post any questions that you might have about the approach, and you'll usually get answers within a day, if not in minutes or hours. Also, many folks on this message board have come up with or are still tinkering with new and interesting variations on the approach.

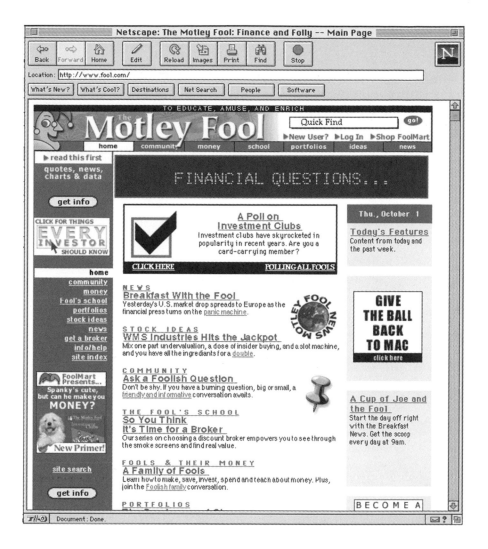

For basic and detailed information on any stock, head over to our high-powered quote server. It's at http://quote. fool.com (you can reach it via the navigation bar on the left of our main screen at http://www.fool.com). Just type in as many tickers as you want, click "Get Info," and bingo – you'll be staring at a wealth of information. By selecting the "Detailed" instead of "Simple" presentation option, you'll find both dividend yields and annual dollar amounts of dividends.

Do You Have Enough Money to Start?

If you've saved $185 and are eager to begin investing with the Dow Approach, you might want to cool your jets a bit until you save a little more moola. That you've begun to save money at all is, of course, Foolish and commendable, but to realistically begin using the Dow approach you need a certain amount of the green stuff — but it's not much, so don't fret.

What's the minimum amount required to begin investing in this strategy? Well, it depends chiefly on how many stocks you'll be buying and how much you'll be paying in brokerage commissions for each trade you make.

You don't want the brokerage commissions that you pay to represent more than about 2% of your investment, at most. For example, if you're buying $500 of each stock and your commission is $40, you're forking over 8% of your investment in commissions. That means you're 8% behind from the start. That's not good. If you plan to invest with the High-Yield Ten approach, you'll be paying commissions on the purchases of ten different stocks, so your total commissions paid will be extra steep. Those with limited funds should probably start with a four-stock variation, as there will be fewer commissions involved.

Beyond that, seriously consider using a discount broker if you're not already doing so. Full-service brokers ("full-price brokers," as we like to call them) almost always charge much higher commissions than their discount brethren. The high fees are justified, they argue, because the brokerages offer advice and recommendations. But Fools do their own homework and make their own decisions (often topping the performance of the high-priced pros). A discount broker that simply executes orders for a low commission is all that's needed -- especially for the Dow Approach, where the system automatically selects which stocks you buy or sell.

Discount brokerages that offer online trading are now advertising commissions of $9 to $12 per trade, and sometimes even lower. If you're paying $12 to buy a stock, you can buy just $600 worth of stock and the commission will only represent 2% of your trade. (12 divided by 600 = 2%.) With a four-stock approach, if you have about $2500, you can start investing. To find more information about discount brokers, visit the Fool's Discount Brokerage Center on the Internet at http://www.fool.com/media/DiscountBrokerageCenter/DiscountBrokerageCenter.htm

Now that's one long address! Somebody should be fired for making it so long! The handy information that it provides makes up for it, though.

What to Do With Dividends

Throughout the year, the stocks you own will pay dividends on a quarterly basis. What should you do with these dividends? It's probably easiest just to let the dividends accrue in your brokerage cash account until you make your annual portfolio adjustment. The returns for the Dow Approach variations covered here assume that dividends sit idle until the annual adjustment. Of course, if you put them into a brokerage money market account they will gain some interest while you wait to invest them at portfolio adjustment time.

Reallocating After Each Round

You picked the Dow Approach variation that you like best. You bought the stocks. You've held for at least a year and a day. (There's more on holding periods later — we promise!) It's time to reallocate so that you're holding the right Dow stocks again. How do you do that? There's a little math involved — mostly just to divvy up what we hope is your larger pile of money after a year. You'll divvy that up in order to even out the amount of money that you invest in each stock as you renew the approach for another year.

For example, what began as a total investment of $20,000 divided into four stocks (with $5,000 in each), may be worth $24,000 after being invested for one year. You might now have, say, $5,500 worth of one stock, $6,200 worth of another, and so on. If that's the case, you've got some adjusting to do. You'll need to start off this new round of the Dow Approach by investing equal dollar amounts again in your new group of stocks. With a $24,000 total investment and four selected stocks, this means putting $6,000 in each. Pretty easy stuff.

To reallocate your portfolio:

1. Take the total dollar value of your portfolio — including dividends that you received over the year (which you kept in your account) and any additional money that you want to add to your portfolio — and divide by the total number of Dow Approach stocks that you'll hold for the next cycle.

    The divisor depends on the approach you use. For the Foolish Four and RP4 variations, divide by four because you hold four stocks. For the High-Yield Ten approach, divide by ten because you hold ten stocks. That will give you the target dollar amount to allocate to each stock for the coming year.

2. Get your list of new stocks to buy, either from the Fool's online forum or by crunching the numbers yourself. (Or have a teenager do it for you.) You'll probably find that one or more of your currently held stocks will be on the buy list again. That's perfectly normal.

3. Sell all of the stock that is being replaced — that is, stocks you currently own that don't appear on the new list.

4. If you have stocks that stayed on the new list that you already own from last year, take a look at the dollar value of each of those stock holdings. If the dollar amount is significantly above the amount you must target for each

stock, sell enough shares to bring the dollar amount invested in those stocks down to the general vicinity of your target amount.

For example, perhaps one stock that you'll be keeping for the next year has grown so that your holding is worth $7,000. If, as in the example above, you want to plunk $6,000 in each of your four stocks, you have too much of this stock and will need to sell about $1,000 worth of shares to keep its initial value around $6,000, like the other stocks.

5. If any of the stocks staying on for a second run are significantly below the target value, buy enough additional shares to bring the amount of that holding up to the general vicinity of your target.

    For example, let's say you bought $5,000 worth of one stock in the last round of the Dow Approach, and it is now worth $5,200. Let's also say that this stock remains in the selected list of stocks. You'll want to buy roughly $800 worth of additional shares to make the initial investment worth about $6,000, even with the others.

6. Using the remaining cash, buy the appropriate amount of the new stocks on the list. When you are deciding how many shares to buy, always round down, and make sure that rounding down leaves enough cash in your account to cover commissions.

Don't get carried away with being totally balanced. It makes little sense to buy or sell 3 shares of a company you are keeping for a second year just to make the numbers look nice. We suggest "balancing" only to the extent that you can do so while keeping the commission cost below 2% of your total investment. So if you're paying $10 per trade, you shouldn't bother to rebalance anything within $500 of the target value.

Also remember — this is a mechanical model. In other words, no subjective evaluation on your part is required. In fact, that only serves to hurt the model. All the back-testing and research has been done assuming that the system is followed the same way repeatedly. After the first round, you may have grown very fond of General Electric or Sears or any stock that has performed well for you. But you should stick with the system. If the system says you should sell a particular stock now, sell it – if you are going to follow the system properly. Remember, though, you could still hold these stocks outside of your Dow Approach investments if you wish.

There's no reason you can't keep a particular stock — it just shouldn't remain a part of your Dow Approach portfolio. Note that once you're investing outside the Dow Approach, you're suddenly the one making the decisions, not the mechanical system. This means that you'll have to do some homework on your holdings, and follow them and their progress. Don't hold any stock blindly or without reason.

 ## When to Start

In our online forum, one of the most frequently asked questions about the Dow Approach has to do with what time of year is the best time to start using the approach. The question comes up because the end of the calendar year and the beginning of a new year coincide with times when large institutional investors (i.e., mutual funds) do some "window dressing." Window dressing means buying and selling stocks so that the end-of-year holdings that will be listed in annual reports to shareholders are impressive. Window dressing and other factors (the reconfiguring of portfolios in general each year, in part for tax purposes) have historically resulted in a seasonal boost for the stock market in January, commonly referred to as the "January Effect." Some argue that this is now a self-fulfilling prophecy – although many times it seems that it doesn't quite "self-fulfill."

Anyway, does it matter whether you begin investing with the Dow Approach in January or July? Well, we did some digging in our monster database to find out.

The most striking thing we found when we looked at the average annual return for portfolios that started at various times during the year was that there does indeed appear to be a decidedly seasonal bias. Specifically, we looked at portfolios starting the first trading day of each month and holding for one year, renewing, and so on for 25 years. The statistical results were quite clear — over time, the January portfolio significantly outperformed all others, followed closely by December.

Here are the annualized 25-year returns for the High-Yield Ten, Foolish Four, and RP4 variations beginning in different months.

Starting Month	HY10	Foolish Four	RP4
Jan.	17.69%	21.86%	24.62%
Feb.	16.07%	17.18%	18.66%
Mar.	16.35%	17.52%	19.06%
Apr.	15.85%	15.03%	15.30%
May	15.50%	17.84%	17.30%
June	15.61%	15.80%	15.04%
July	16.40%	13.87%	15.58%
Aug.	17.09%	18.22%	16.47%
Sep.	15.63%	16.53%	17.53%
Oct.	16.07%	16.81%	17.52%
Nov.	16.42%	16.66%	19.31%
Dec.	17.42%	19.21%	22.05%

While these results support the argument that starting these Dow Approach strategies in December or on the first trading day in January has an advantage in terms of higher returns, please bear in mind that this doesn't tell you anything about what will happen this year — or next. A statistical average is not for predicting short-term results, nor even long-term ones, for that matter. It is only an indication of what might happen based on what has happened in the past. There were years when the returns using a July or August start date outperformed those when starting in January. In addition, 13.87% returns for the Foolish Four renewing in July is not a bad return — it's notably better than the S&P 500 and the Dow 30 over that period. But over time, the historical record points to mid-December or the first trading day in January as the optimal starting period.

Why do we say mid-December or early January? Why not just January 1st? (Okay, maybe January 2nd since the market is closed on January 1st, which, of course, has nothing to do with the lingering effects of New Year's Eve.) Well, for investors who hold their Dow Approach stocks in a tax-advantaged account such as an IRA, it is clear that the first trading day of the year is the winner based on the data we have now. But for those who have to contend with capital gains taxes, the picture is just a little bit muddier — it ain't no Louisiana bayou, though.

In order to qualify for the lower long-term capital gains tax rate, it is essential that stocks be held for one year and a day. That being the case, one cannot renew one's Dow Approach stocks on the same day each year. And since returns drop off somewhat steeply towards February, it looks like starting sometime in the middle of December, and then renewing a year and a day later each year, would be the best course of action to take.

Even so, eventually, the renewal date will start creeping through January and maybe into February (remember, this is a long-term approach). If this happens, our suggestion is to use the occasional bad year (and they will happen) to shift the renewal date back. For example, one year you may be looking at a very small gain or even a loss around the middle of December. Consider reconfiguring your investments early and taking a short-term capital gain (or loss) to move your renewal date back to mid-December or the first trading day in January.

What if you're ready to start now, but it's nowhere near December or January? You want to optimize your potential returns, but do you need to wait until mid-December or early January to do that? What if you start now (say it's August) and then renew on January 2?

We looked at the results of starting each month from February to November and holding only until the end of the year. The average returns were fair, but the results were so varied that it appeared you had an equal chance of making or losing money, and if you made money, you would have to pay taxes at the steep short-term capital gains rate! So beginning mid-year and flipping out early to reconfigure in December or January is not particularly attractive.

Then we tried buying in months other than January and holding through the end of the current year all the way to the end of the following year. Ahhhh! Now we're getting somewhere. The results (on an annualized basis) were just a bit lower than the average results for the strategy as a whole, but much more consistent. Again, the statistics don't say anything about what will happen this year or next, but of all the choices for starting at a time other than December or January, this strategy appears to be the most statistically attractive. So, for example, if you're starting in March of 1998, you'd hold past January of 1999 and not renew/reallocate until mid-December of 1999 or the first trading day in January of 2000.

The Holding Period

Our research has shown that holding your Dow Approach portfolio for a year and a day before reallocating is the most effective holding period (and it takes advantage of the lower long-term capital gains tax rate for taxable accounts). So considering the seasonal factors and the optimal holding period, what are the bottom-line recommendations we can make?

1. Set up your portfolio to renew in late December or by the first trading day of the year.

2. Hold for one year and a day. (For portfolios held in tax-deferred and tax-free accounts, you can hold for just one year.)

3. When your stocks have a less-than-stellar year, use that as the time to back up your renewal date to keep in the mid-December/first trading day of January zone if need be.

4. You can start the strategy at any time, but hold your first portfolio through the end of the year and renew the following mid-December or on the first trading day of January. In the long run, you're holding for one year and a day with each cycle. ◆

Part 3

TAX CONSIDERATIONS

TAX CONSIDERATIONS

Taxes affect everyone's investment returns. Imagine that you sell a stock that has increased in value by 12% and your gain is $600. Come tax time, Uncle Sam will take a bite out of that — perhaps as much as $200 or more. However, let's say that your tax on that gain was just $120. That leaves you with a gain of $480 and a net return of just 9.6%. Before the tax you had a return that topped the 11% historical average annual return of the stock market, but after taxes you're well below that benchmark.

How much you pay in taxes on investment gains and when you pay those taxes can have a large impact on your total return over the long haul. But there are some steps that you can take to minimize your tax burden while using the Dow Approach.

For starters, consider the type of account you are using for your Dow Approach portfolio. There are three main categories of investment accounts: taxable accounts, tax-deferred accounts, and Roth IRAs. Taxable accounts include regular brokerage accounts. In these, you put in as much money as you want anytime, buy stocks, sell stocks, and pay taxes on the capital gains and dividends every year. Tax-deferred accounts include IRAs, SEP IRAs, Keoghs, and 401(k) plans, where you don't pay taxes on gains in the account until you begin to withdraw money, ideally at retirement. Roth IRAs are a bit different — while the money you contribute to the Roth IRA is not tax-deductible (it's after-tax money), the gains you make in your Roth account accumulate tax-free. When you eventually make qualified withdrawals from your Roth IRA, you will pay no federal income taxes on it.

It makes sense to use the Dow Approach in a tax-deferred account. Not all such accounts permit this — 401(k)s, for example, are typically restricted to mutual funds — but IRAs do. The advantage in an IRA is that you can turn over your portfolio every year as you reconfigure it to hold the latest batch of selected stocks — and postpone or avoid the payment of taxes all the while. In a regular brokerage account, each year that you generate a profit you'll be socked with a tax bill.

Tax-deferred Accounts

If you're investing in a tax-deferred account, holding periods that determine capital gains taxes don't apply. Simply keep records showing the amount of post-tax money you've put into the account(s) so you don't pay taxes on it twice. Everything you earn in these accounts will be taxed as normal income when you take it out at retirement. It'll be taxed at whatever rate is appropriate for your tax bracket at that time. Since your gains accumulate tax-deferred, this is a great investment vehicle in which to use the Dow Approach.

Taxable Accounts and Capital Gains

If you're investing with the Dow Approach in a regular, taxable account, you need to give thought to capital gains and the taxes levied on them. Capital gains are the profits earned from capital assets (such as stocks) that you have sold, minus any losses from unprofitable sales (losses) of capital assets.

Capital gains currently come in two flavors: long-term and short-term. Short-term capital gains (defined as those held one year or less) carry a higher tax rate than long-term gains. In fact, the short-term rate is the same as your ordinary income tax rate. So if you're in the top tax bracket, you'll pay a steep rate on any short-term gains. The long-term capital gains rate applies to any stocks held for more than a year and is 20% for most folks. (Those in the 15% tax bracket pay only 10%.)

Since the Dow Approach has you buying and selling stocks roughly once a year, you need to be aware of the tax laws for capital gains to keep your tax bite to a minimum. The secret, of course, is to make sure that you hold those stocks for at least a year and a day if there are any gains involved in order to qualify for the lower long-term capital gains tax rate.

Have we stressed that year-and-a-day thing enough yet? No? One more time, you say? Well, then, remember — stocks held for just 365 days will generate a short-term gain or loss, which means that you might end up paying up to twice as much in taxes as you would if you waited that extra day. So hold those horses in the stable that one extra day.

In a taxable account, you will also have to pay taxes on the dividends you receive, which are taxed at your normal income tax rate.

Future Changes and More Information

As American citizens know too well, tax laws are constantly changing. For the latest on tax law developments, check out the IRS's website at http://www.irs.ustreas.gov. It offers complete tax information, including downloadable tax forms and instructions. Or, if you're not online, give the IRS a call for the latest on tax laws and forms regarding capital gains and losses. You're also invited to join us online in our tax area. Here the Fool offers a message board where you can post questions and get answers, as well as detailed information on Roth IRAs, wash sales, capital gains taxes, and much more. You might also want to check out our *Motley Fool Investment Tax Guide*, available from FoolMart (http://www.foolmart.com) or call 1-888-665-FOOL, or your local bookstore.

Finally, we recommend consulting a tax professional to evaluate your personal tax situation whenever you have doubts. Everyone's taxes are different and the laws differ from state to state. Our tax area is designed to be a starting point for tax issues and is aimed at a general audience. It's not intended to be personalized tax advice for individuals. ◆

Part 4

THE PRINCIPLES BEHIND THE APPROACH

THE PRINCIPLES BEHIND THE APPROACH

Buying Big Brand Names

Since the Dow Jones Industrial Average was created in 1896, the purpose of the index has been to measure the American economy and the overall stock market through a group of select, world-leading companies. The people creating and updating the index work to keep it current, relevant, and representative of the economy as a whole. It's meant to track some of the best American companies and, therefore, holds only large, multinational, and industry-leading firms.

You'll certainly recognize most of the 30 companies in the Dow Jones Industrial Average (see the Appendix for a complete list, current as of September 1998). In fact, you likely use many of these companies' products on a daily basis. For example, does the name AT&T ring a bell? Have you ever had a Coke and a smile? And we suspect that you've heard of a little car company named General Motors. Among the 30 Dow Jones Industrial Average stocks, you'll find other familiar names, including Walt Disney, McDonald's, Johnson & Johnson, and General Electric.

There are no small companies in the Dow Jones family. In fact, no company on the list has a market capitalization (total market value) of less than five billion dollars. The lowest-valued company on the Dow at the time of this writing was Union Carbide, with a market cap of $5.17 billion. As of

September 1998, the 30 Dow companies had a total combined market value of $1.98 trillion, an average value of $66 billion per company.

Just how well known and respected are the companies that you buy using the Dow Approach? Let's take a quick look at a few Dow stocks.

AT&T. The leading long-distance telephone provider in the world was founded more than 100 years ago and has been a part of the Dow Jones Industrial Average since 1939. Even after the spin-off of its seven "Baby Bells," AT&T is still the largest telecommunications company in the world — well ahead of numbers two and three in long-distance, MCI WorldCom and Sprint.

At the time of this writing, AT&T has $51 billion in sales over the previous twelve months, or 45% more than MCI and Sprint combined. AT&T controls more than 50% of the long-distance market and, in 1997, the company spent about $9 billion to expand its network, including a focus on local phone services and Internet services.

AT&T has a brand name as strong as any company in the country and it owns the largest phone network in the world. The company employs more than 120,000 people.

Coca-Cola. The Coca-Cola Company has consistently grown the value of its business since it was founded in 1886. It became a public company in 1919, and since that time the stock has had an annualized return of more than 16% (with dividends reinvested). Over eighty years, that rate of return turned $40 (the price of one share of Coke's stock in 1919) into nearly $5.7 million. (No, you didn't read that incorrectly.) More recently, from 1980 to 1997, Coca-Cola's share price grew a sizzling 24% annually, creating an additional $90 billion in wealth for Coca-Cola shareholders.

Coca-Cola is the world's leading soft drink company, recently holding 44% of the U.S. market and 48% of the international market. The company's products represent four of the top ten most popular beverages in the world, with

Coca-Cola Classic leading the bunch. Coke sells its products in more than 200 countries and is continually expanding distribution. Coke is also a leading provider of juice products, owning brand names such as Minute Maid.

The company has the most popular brand name in the world valued at an estimated $50 billion alone. Coke had more than $18 billion in sales in 1997 and, at the time of this writing, is the second-highest-valued stock of the Dow 30 based on market cap, behind only General Electric. Coca-Cola is perhaps the ideal example of the "big brand name" companies that make up the Dow Jones Industrial Average. Wall Street loves this stock, though, so the dividend yield is not likely to become high enough to make Coke qualify for the Dow Approach. Instead, many Fools buy some of this stock outside of their Dow Approach holdings to keep for ten years or longer.

General Motors. GM was formed in the early 1920s, when the world's leading car maker — Ford Motor Company — was still making only identical cars. World War I had recently ended, and Americans wanted their purchases to reflect their individual personalities. General Motors seized that opportunity and began manufacturing different types and colors of cars. By 1927, the company surpassed Ford in total sales and, since then, General Motors has been the leading car company in the country and in the world.

General Motors sells more cars than Ford and Chrysler combined, with $166 billion in sales for 1997. The company employs approximately 608,000 people. General Motors is a name known around the world — from Japan, to South America, to Africa.

When you buy Dow stocks, either separately or through the Dow Approach, you're purchasing some of the largest, most respected, and well-known companies not only in the country, but on the planet. From the leading entertainment giant, to the largest oil and gas companies, to the dominant fast-food chain, the Dow stocks represent some of the biggest and best brands that you can buy.

This is one of the primary factors behind the long-term success of this investment approach. Most mechanical investment models have you investing in small companies, many that you've never heard of, based on various (and often confusing) screening techniques. The simple Dow Approach keeps your money in high quality, time-proven companies. It bears repeating — buying these giant names under the Dow Approach has resulted in returns that trounce the market averages. This is hard for novice investors to believe — those who think they must find new, small, fast-growing companies to make market-beating returns — but it's true.

Dividends Matter

Sometime in the 1980s, investors stopped worrying about dividends.

Long considered a badge of honor on Wall Street, paying a dividend was a sign that a company had arrived. Giving investors a quarterly lump of cash and being listed on the New York Stock Exchange (NYSE) virtually accorded a company the status of nobility. Receiving dividend income from your investments was as important as expecting capital appreciation over the longer term. Investors would proudly say to one another that they did not invest in a company unless it paid a dividend. Pension funds, for the most part, still bear the marks of that era, as many to this day cannot invest in a stock unless it offers a quarterly dividend payout.

Fast-forward to the late 1990s. The dividend yield on the S&P 500 stands at a paltry 1.88% (in late 1998), well below the historical level. Paying out shareholder earnings in the form of stock dividends is now frowned upon by many professional investors, who complain that dividends are taxed twice (once when the company earns it as income and again when shareholders receive it as income). Better to spend the money repurchasing stock or expanding the business rather than putting a tax burden on investors. With the massive shift to professionally managed money in the form of mutual funds, most managers tend to ignore the dividend pay-out altogether. With these folks focused firmly on outperforming the market over the next six to eighteen months, dividend yield pales in comparison to the 20% or better capital appreciation numbers they are chasing.

Dow Approach investors know better. They know that dividends matter.

Think of it this way. Statistics tells us that the Dow Jones Industrial Average, as a whole, has about a 0.80 correlation with the S&P 500. As the 30 Dow stocks represent approximately 26% of the market capitalization of the S&P 500 as of late 1998, it is no surprise that both indexes tend to behave the same way. Although a selection of four to ten Dow stocks will probably have a lower correlation to the performance of the S&P 500, overall they will have a much higher correlation than almost any other small group of stocks, because Dow stocks represent such a large part of the index.

So any group of Dow stocks and the S&P 500 as a whole tend to perform roughly in line with one another over time. What does this mean? Quite a bit, if you are concerned with the total return (dividend yield and capital appreciation) on your investments. If you look at the dividend yield in addition to capital appreciation, on a total-return basis there is absolutely no surprise as to why the Dow Approach beats the S&P 500 hands-down over time. By cherry-picking four to ten of the highest-yielding companies of the S&P 500, you get all the performance of the S&P 500 plus a dividend yield that, on average, is about 50% higher than that of the S&P 500. This translates into a 1% to 3% better total return each year, on average, which compounded over time means that the total return will be substantially greater.

For a moment, set aside the idea that the Dow Approach gets you into large companies that have been dumped due to short-term bad news or allows you to buy into cyclical companies at their low points. The simple fact is that because you buy a group of stocks that tend to perform in line with the S&P 500 and then also get a better dividend yield, you are probably going to beat the S&P 500's total return. Although, in the short-term, a dividend may appear paltry, over long periods of time the compounding effect of the dividend yield can leave investors with a significantly better total return, even if they have only performed in-line with the index.

Contrarian Investing

Ninety percent of the employed population works during day-time hours. Suppose that you're offered a new job and are given the choice to work either a daytime or nighttime shift. You weigh the options. You consider that most people work during the day and, as a result, the highways are crowded with traffic in the mornings and late afternoons. You further consider how crowded grocery stores and restaurants are in the evenings. You realize that if you worked nights, you could avoid the highway traffic, have the days to shop in less crowded stores, and eat good lunches at quiet restaurants for much lower prices than are charged at dinner time. On top of this, you get paid more at your new job if you work the later shift.

You decide that the night shift is advantageous for you so you choose it. This is an example of a contrarian action — you're acting differently than the majority, and you're benefiting in many ways as a result.

Likewise, there are contrarians in the investing world. In fact, people are often schooled on the advantages of being a contrarian investor. The argument is this: If you're buying a stock at the same time that everyone else is buying that stock, you're paying a higher price than you'd otherwise need to, as the current mass of buyers is pushing the price higher. Similarly, if you're selling while everyone else is selling, theoretically you'll get a lower price for your shares, because the selling pushes the price down.

If you do the opposite — if you're contrarian and you buy when everyone else is selling and sell when everyone else is buying — in the process you should receive more attractive prices on both ends. This sounds brilliant on paper, but it's extremely difficult in practice with individual stocks... at least, it is until you employ the Dow Approach.

There are two variables that help the Dow Approach work so well:

1. The companies you buy are paying the highest dividends in the Dow (and often in the entire stock market).

2. The stock price of these companies is usually lower than normal because the high dividend yield that we just mentioned is due in part to a lower-than-normal stock price. (Again, these two factors combined make for a Dow Approach stock.)

When a company falls out of favor (as, for example, AT&T did for much of the 1990s following sweeping industry changes and intense competition), the stock price will decline and the dividend yield will rise. At any given time, the Dow Approach leads you invest in the lowest-priced and highest-yielding (yet, for some reason, usually the least sought after) Dow stocks. You're buying while others are selling and you're receiving not only an attractive dividend yield, but a decent share price as well. You've bought "low," as they say. What's next?

Ideally, once your twelve-month-and-a-day holding period is complete, the story behind your Dow Approach stocks has changed (hopefully it has improved), your stocks are selling at much higher prices (people have been buying them), and the dividend yield is lower. This is typically when the approach has you sell your holdings (when many others are buying) and move into the latest high-yielding, beaten-down Dow stocks.

But can such a simple investment method continue to work once everyone knows about it? (Admittedly, this method has grown in popularity tremendously over the past five years.) How can it continue to work? The following section addresses why we think it can.

Why and How It Works

Many investors are skeptical whether the historical market-beating returns generated by the Dow Approach are sustainable. Those who believe the approach is doomed to obsolescence might not fully appreciate how the approach marries the pursuit of dividend income and stock price appreciation. The Dow Approach creates a portfolio focused on total return, not simply dividend income (income) or price appreciation (growth). Dow investors get the best of both worlds.

When you buy stocks using the Dow Approach, two things happen. First, as we've explained, you purchase stocks with a higher-than-average dividend yield. Second, you buy a basket of securities that will probably contain one or two members that have fallen victim to Wall Street's tendency to overreact to bad news.

You need both dividend yield and capital appreciation (a rising stock price) to have a solid total return. Any company that pays out the majority of its income in the form of dividends (like an electric utility) will probably see very little capital appreciation in the foreseeable future. However, yield is important to overall returns. More than 3% of the S&P 500's approximately 11% average annual return since 1926 has come from dividends — that's almost 30% of the total return. However tax-disadvantaged receiving dividends may be, you leave a big chunk of the total return on the table if you choose to ignore them.

When you buy a group of stocks with an above-average yield, you increase your chances of beating the market significantly. Over long periods of time, if the stocks go up as much as the market, you will beat the market on a total-return basis because the stocks have a higher-than-average dividend yield.

Yield may also be a superior way to identify companies that have been mispriced by the market. Unlike strategies that look at price momentum, earnings momentum, or current valuation based on sales or earnings, a yield-based price screen is almost immune from tampering or cyclical fluctuations. Earnings and sales, over time, are subject to accounting concerns and are rather volatile, particularly for a cyclical industry. However, a dividend yield is a dividend yield. There aren't many ways to fake an investor into thinking he got a larger dividend than was actually paid. Because yield is logically related to price, any yield-based strategy will automatically leave out stocks that have had significant price momentum because no company raises its dividend payout more than once or twice a year. Additionally, yield is real money in someone's pocket – it is not some abstract number that merely serves as a guide to valuation.

Unlike almost any other index, a Dow stock with a high yield is almost assuredly a growing company that has been knocked down in price recently due to some news event. Although the Dow Approach hardly captures all Dow stocks that are mispriced because of short-term concerns, even getting one out of every four or five can add a couple of points to long-term returns. At the very least, your high-yielding portfolio will not contain stocks that have had their prices explode in the last few months, as a high-yielder on the Dow has almost always already come under selling pressure. By mixing potential mispricing with a higher-than-average yield, Dow Approach investors have done spankingly well over the last 25 years, netting a compound annual growth rate of between 17.69% and 24.62%, depending on the specific variation.

 ### Long-term Perseverance Makes Up for Losing Years

You must be aware, though, that there will be years where the approach doesn't perform as well. The real strength of this investment strategy is its long-term results. Just as you can't cherry-pick "star" mutual funds, your crystal ball probably won't give you a very clear picture of what years will be winners and what years will be losers for the stock market. We can't predict the future, but we can look at what happened to the Dow Approach strategies in the past. While past performance is never a guarantee of future results, it gives the best clue we can get to them.

Jim O'Shaughnessy, author of *What Works on Wall Street*, has calculated returns since 1928 on two popular Dow Approach variations that he calls the "Dogs of the Dow" (the High-Yield Ten and High-Yield Five). In the Great Depression years (1928 — 1930) they were crushed with the rest of the market — down to about a third of their pre-Depression value. But both sprang back quickly. By the end of 1936, both approaches were showing a profit.

The Dow Approach has provided market-beating results over the long haul. That's why it's important to adopt a long-term focus for these investment strategies. On average, looking at historical returns, the Dow Approach tends to protect you on the downside, but often doesn't perform as well in very strong bull markets like we've had over the past three or four years. It does well, sometimes outstandingly well, in individual years such as 1995 when the RP4 variation clocked in with a 47.05% return compared to 37.43% for the S&P 500 and 36.69% for the Dow 30. Conversely, in 1997 the S&P 500 was the clear winner, beating the Dow 30 and all the Dow Approach variations by more than 10 percentage points.

What if you have the worst luck in the world? Say you picked the worst possible time to invest in the last 35 years. That has to include 1973–1974. An investment in the Dow 30 lost 10.86% in 1973 and then 15.64% in 1974, while the S&P 500 lost 14.66% and 26.47%. In that same period, the Foolish Four made money — 25.74% in 1973 and 5.25% in 1974. The High-Yield Ten was up nearly 5% over the same period. That's not so bad, is it? There's no guarantee, of course. In the bear market of 1990, all the strategies went down. But, if you are willing to leave your money in the market for more than five years, based on historical returns, the odds you'll beat the market averages are heavily in your favor.

Many of our real-money online portfolios at The Motley Fool utilize the Dow Approach, but only with a portion of the portfolio (usually 25%). This strategy provides a base of stable, market-beating investments in large companies to balance out any unusual risk we might take in other stocks. That is another way you might want to utilize these approaches for your own portfolio.

 ## Some Final Supporting Evidence (Rolling Averages)

"Rolling averages" are a very powerful way to tell if an investment strategy is really sound or is the result of some fluke. With rolling averages, you don't just look at the returns over a single specific time period. Instead, you look at returns over multiple, overlapping time periods.

Here's how they work. If you hold a stock for 10 years, your average return over that period is clearly a 10-year average. However, you also have two 9-year averages — one starting the year you bought the stock, and one starting the next year. These two 9-year averages overlap. If you look at 5-year periods during those 10 years, you have six overlapping 5-year periods: Years 1–5, 2–6, 3–7, 4–8, 5–9 and 6–10.

So why are these rolling returns important? If a strategy is really sound, you would expect it to work well during most of those 5-year periods. For example, if a certain strategy's returns were the result of, say, one amazing year where every stock tripled in price, and if someone bought in after that one year... tough luck.

Looking at these rolling averages lets you see how you would have done starting the strategy in any year since 1963. The tables that follow present 5-year, 10-year, 20-year, and 25-year rolling averages for the High-Yield 10, Foolish Four, and RP4 strategies over the 35-year period from 1963 to 1997.

As you can see from the 5-year rolling returns table, there are thirty-one 5-year periods in the last 35 years. Take a look, because the numbers are impressive. For the three strategies we discuss in this book, only one 5-year period in the last 35 years shows a loss: The RP4 lost 0.78% from 1966–70. That period was also the only period where the S&P 500 beat our Dow Approach strategies. In every other 5-year period, the best strategy was either the Foolish Four or the RP4 variation.

If you like numbers, compare the volatility of the year-to-year returns shown in the table in Appendix B with the much smoother 5-year averages.

And think about this — suppose the worst had happened and you jumped into the Foolish Four strategy in 1966. In the very first year your stocks lost 17.65%, the single worst year for the Foolish Four. If you had hung in there even after this awful start, the 5-year period that began following that disaster (1967–1971) returned an average of 11.07% per year for the Foolish Four — and incidentally, beat the other strategies by almost 3 percentage points. ◆

Rolling Returns: 5-Year Rolling Average Annual Returns

	High-Yield 10	Foolish Four	RP4	S&P500	Dow 30
1963–67	12.39%	14.19%	12.11%	12.39%	11.96%
1964–68	11.18%	13.54%	12.06%	10.16%	9.51%
1965–69	4.26%	6.79%	5.36%	4.97%	3.92%
1966–70	1.57%	3.06%	-0.78%	3.34%	1.64%
1967–71	6.84%	11.07%	8.34%	8.42%	6.87%
1968–72	6.51%	8.43%	5.36%	7.53%	5.96%
1969–73	4.43%	10.55%	5.17%	2.01%	1.58%
1970–74	7.54%	13.24%	11.01%	-2.35%	0.11%
1971–75	15.89%	27.27%	27.08%	3.21%	6.67%
1972–76	21.38%	30.73%	30.73%	4.87%	10.37%
1973–77	16.58%	26.35%	26.02%	-0.21%	4.17%
1974–78	16.25%	22.99%	24.39%	4.32%	7.13%
1975–79	18.18%	22.26%	23.91%	14.76%	13.24%
1976–80	15.03%	19.13%	16.54%	13.95%	10.09%
1977–81	9.65%	10.82%	11.32%	8.08%	3.87%
1978–82	13.62%	17.57%	22.54%	14.05%	10.63%
1979–83	20.67%	23.71%	28.02%	17.27%	16.95%
1980–84	20.18%	25.61%	26.37%	14.76%	14.43%
1981–85	19.75%	20.98%	31.20%	14.71%	15.45%
1982–86	24.90%	28.18%	35.67%	19.87%	20.92%
1983–87	22.24%	23.75%	28.13%	16.49%	20.13%
1984–88	18.39%	18.39%	25.26%	15.38%	16.03%
1985–89	22.92%	19.46%	32.73%	20.40%	22.67%
1986–90	14.10%	10.28%	17.77%	13.14%	14.02%
1987–91	15.10%	18.41%	18.69%	15.36%	15.57%
1988–92	14.63%	20.56%	21.02%	15.89%	14.57%
1989–93	15.70%	23.12%	22.60%	14.51%	15.39%
1990–94	10.37%	20.78%	15.13%	8.69%	9.97%
1991–95	20.07%	32.40%	29.27%	16.57%	19.33%
1992–96	18.65%	22.74%	27.65%	15.20%	18.20%
1993–97	21.63%	21.26%	25.53%	20.24%	20.52%

10-Year Rolling Average Annual Returns

	High-Yield 10	Foolish Four	RP4	S&P500	Dow 30
1963–72	9.41%	11.27%	8.68%	9.93%	8.92%
1964–73	7.75%	12.04%	8.56%	6.01%	5.47%
1965–74	5.89%	9.97%	8.15%	1.24%	2.00%
1966–75	8.49%	14.53%	12.29%	3.27%	4.13%
1967–76	13.88%	20.50%	19.01%	6.63%	8.60%
1968–77	11.43%	17.04%	15.23%	3.59%	5.06%
1969–78	10.18%	16.61%	14.38%	3.16%	4.32%
1970–79	12.74%	17.66%	17.28%	5.86%	6.47%
1971–80	15.46%	23.13%	21.70%	8.44%	8.37%
1972–81	15.37%	20.36%	20.63%	6.47%	7.07%
1973–82	15.09%	21.88%	24.27%	6.68%	7.35%
1974–83	18.44%	23.35%	26.19%	10.61%	11.93%
1975–84	19.17%	23.92%	25.13%	14.76%	13.84%
1976–85	17.37%	20.05%	23.65%	14.33%	12.74%
1977–86	17.03%	19.18%	22.89%	13.82%	12.07%
1978–87	17.85%	20.62%	25.31%	15.26%	15.28%
1979–88	19.53%	21.02%	26.63%	16.33%	16.49%
1980–89	21.54%	22.49%	29.51%	17.55%	18.48%
1981–90	16.89%	15.51%	24.30%	13.93%	14.74%
1982–91	19.90%	23.19%	26.90%	17.59%	18.21%
1983–92	18.38%	22.14%	24.53%	16.19%	17.32%
1984–93	17.04%	20.73%	23.93%	14.94%	15.71%
1985–94	16.48%	20.11%	23.62%	14.40%	16.15%
1986–95	17.04%	20.84%	23.39%	14.84%	16.64%
1987–96	16.87%	20.55%	23.09%	15.28%	16.88%
1988–97	18.08%	20.91%	23.25%	18.05%	17.51%

20-Year Rolling Average Annual Returns

	High-Yield 10	Foolish Four	RP4	S&P500	Dow 30
1963–82	12.21%	16.45%	16.21%	8.30%	8.13%
1964–83	12.97%	17.56%	17.04%	8.28%	8.65%
1965–84	12.33%	16.74%	16.33%	7.79%	7.75%
1966–85	12.84%	17.26%	17.83%	8.66%	8.35%
1967–86	15.44%	19.84%	20.94%	10.17%	10.32%
1968–87	14.60%	18.82%	20.16%	9.27%	10.05%
1969–88	14.76%	18.79%	20.35%	9.55%	10.23%
1970–89	17.06%	20.05%	23.24%	11.55%	12.32%
1971–90	16.17%	19.26%	22.99%	11.15%	11.51%
1972–91	17.61%	21.77%	23.73%	11.89%	12.50%
1973–92	16.72%	22.01%	24.40%	11.33%	12.22%
1974–93	17.74%	22.03%	25.05%	12.76%	13.80%
1975–94	17.82%	22.00%	24.37%	14.58%	14.99%
1976–95	17.20%	20.44%	23.52%	14.59%	14.68%
1977–96	16.95%	19.86%	22.99%	14.55%	14.45%
1978–97	17.97%	20.76%	24.28%	16.65%	16.39%

25-Year Rolling Average Annual Returns

	High-Yield 10	Foolish Four	RP4	S&P500	Dow 30
1963–87	14.15%	17.88%	18.51%	9.89%	10.43%
1964–88	14.03%	17.72%	18.64%	9.67%	10.09%
1965–89	14.38%	17.28%	19.44%	10.20%	10.58%
1966–90	13.09%	15.83%	17.82%	9.54%	9.46%
1967–91	15.37%	19.55%	20.48%	11.19%	11.35%
1968–92	14.60%	19.16%	20.33%	10.56%	10.94%
1969–93	14.95%	19.65%	20.80%	10.52%	11.25%
1970–94	15.69%	20.20%	21.58%	10.97%	11.84%
1971–95	16.94%	21.78%	24.22%	12.21%	13.03%
1972–96	17.82%	21.96%	24.50%	12.55%	13.62%
1973–97	17.69%	21.86%	24.62%	13.06%	13.83%

Part 5

A HISTORY OF THE DOW

A HISTORY
OF THE DOW

For those who just can't read enough about the marvelous Dow Approach, we end our book with a section on the history of the Dow — the index of stocks upon which the entire approach is founded. It's not only interesting material, but it also will help you understand exactly what newscasters are really referring to each night when they report, "The Dow was up 45 points today."

 Charles Dow, Wall Street Revolutionary

Charles Dow came from humble origins, yet managed to transform the world of investing more than any high-powered money manager or investment banker. He wasn't born in the center of cosmopolitan New York City and he wasn't a financial child prodigy. Dow was born in 1851 on a farm in Connecticut. He worked odd, menial-labor jobs from the age of six to help support his family after the death of his father. Although writing appealed to Dow, he did not finish secondary school. Despite this, at the age of eighteen he managed to get a job as a reporter for *The Springfield Daily Republican*. The *Republican* was a newspaper of national repute edited by newspaper giant Samuel Bowles, renowned for establishing the credentials of aspiring journalists.

Dow continued his reporting work at another prominent newspaper, *The Providence Journal*, in Rhode Island. He worked under the leadership of George W. Danielson, another outstanding editor of the day. Through a series of articles, Dow established himself as an insightful historian of the local scene with a keen interest in financial affairs. From tracing the corporate transactions of steamship companies to discussing investments in Newport real estate, Dow found that financial reporting not only matched his interests but also suited his temperament.

After a move to New York and a stint with the Kiernan News Agency in 1882, he started Dow Jones & Company with two partners, Edward Jones and Charles Bergstresser. They first published a two-page daily called *The Customer's Afternoon Letter* in early 1883. By 1889, *The Customer's Afternoon Letter* evolved into *The Wall Street Journal*.

The Customer's Afternoon Letter was nothing short of revolutionary. In Dow's time, consolidated stock tables published every day did not exist. Information about a company's balance sheet was rarely published, with managements often attempting to hide and obscure the full value of their company for fear of takeover. The *Letter* not only reported consolidated stock tables, but also made public quarterly and annual information regarding company financials — something only available to insiders before this. Dow's publication leveled the playing field between the Wall Street elite and the individual investor. Companies were not required to file 10-Ks and 10-Qs that all investors could look at until the Securities Act of 1934. So for more than 50 years, the only place where the individual investor could get the straight scoop on company financials was *The Customer's Afternoon Letter* and then *The Wall Street Journal*.

In addition to founding the first daily publication dedicated to the financial world, Dow Jones & Co. was the first to see the need for an index that could be used to gauge the activity of the New York Stock Exchange as a whole. The first Dow Jones index, the precursor to the Dow Jones Averages, included eleven stocks — nine railroad companies, Western Union, and Pacific Mail Steamship. At that time, railroad stocks represented a key growth industry. They were the only shares traded in large volume on the NYSE, and that is why they were chosen. The initial average was simply the price of all eleven stocks added up and divided by the number of companies.

Although Charles Dow never wrote anything that claimed he invented the average and, in fact, never really wrote anything at all about his thoughts on investing, the record left by his contemporaries clearly shows that he was the idea man behind all of Dow Jones & Co.'s endeavors, while his partners managed the employees and kept the books. Dow continued to tweak the list of companies making up his average until his death in 1902. Charles Dow left behind the first market average, a barometer for the general pressure of "the market." The investment world would be a very different place without the kind of reporting and financial disclosure pioneered in *The Wall Street Journal* or the notion of an average used to measure where the broader market was at any given point.

 The Dow Jones Averages

It was not until the spring of 1896 that Dow had developed his ideas to the point where he completely removed the railroad issues from his general market average and created two separate averages — the Industrials and the Railroads. *The Wall Street Journal* started to report a separate Railroad Average as well as an average composed entirely of industrial and natural resource concerns — the Dow Jones Industrial Average (DJIA). Although it first appeared on May 26, 1896, the Industrial Average was not reported in *The Wall Street Journal* on a regular basis until October 7th of the same year. Its starting point was a mere 40.94, a fraction of the near-8,000 level where the DJIA sits as of this writing.

Early on, the DJIA was a dynamic average, changing composition on an almost monthly basis. Because the average was supposed to represent the current business environment, Charles Dow actively sought to include the key industries of his time — sugar, spirits, leather, cordage, tobacco, gas, lead, rubber, coal, iron, and electrical products. This is a far cry from today's DJIA, which is dominated by retailing, oil, technology, pharmaceuticals, and entertainment companies.

The original Industrial Average included names like American Cotton Oil, American Sugar, Distilling & Cattle Feeding, Laclede Gas, National Lead, and U.S. Rubber. Today's average has companies like American Express, Walt Disney, Merck, and United Technologies filling its ranks.

The only company on the original list of Industrials that has managed to endure is General Electric — although it was removed from the Index twice, only to be added back again later. The original Railroad Average was replaced by the more generalized Transportation Average after a number of trucking, airline, and air-shipping concerns were added to it in 1970. These changes included the first Dow stocks to come from the Nasdaq Composite instead of just from the New York Stock Exchange. The last development was the creation of the 15-stock Dow Jones Utilities Average, which made its first appearance in 1929.

Despite public perception to the contrary, the Dow Averages have continued to change in recent years. A new component has been added, on average, every three years since the inception of the DJIA. Although originally it was Charles Dow himself who changed the averages, today Dow Jones & Co. employs a "Keeper of the Dow" to perform this function.

The Keeper of the Dow leads the team of Dow Jones editors who oversee any shifts in the composition of the average. The Keeper's job is to see that periodic adjustments are made to ensure that the average continues to reflect the current business climate, as well as to compensate for mergers and bankruptcies involving Dow stocks. This function has maintained Charles Dow's original commitment to ensure that the mix of companies in the average remains analogous to the broader market.

A number of factors are considered when choosing a company to represent a specific industry in the Dow. Is the company a leader? How long has it been around? Does it treat its shareholders well? What is its reputation in its industry? Dow companies have to be leaders in a particular industry or sector. The Dow has traditionally been made up of corporate giants, massive companies whose shares have been publicly traded for decades.

An example of the logic used to maintain the weighting of the Dow is illustrated by the changes that were made in 1985 after Dow component General Foods was bought out by tobacco giant Philip Morris. The sudden addition of Philip Morris to the average upset the industry weighting by doubling the number of tobacco companies (American Brands, formerly American Tobacco was already there). As a result, the Keeper of the Dow decided to drop American Brands entirely and add McDonald's to the Industrial Average to better represent the restaurant industry. The most recent spate of changes was made in 1997, when Woolworth, Bethlehem Steel, Westinghouse, and Texaco were kicked out in order to make room for Wal-Mart, Hewlett-Packard, Johnson & Johnson, and Travelers Group. The last change before that had come in the early 1980s when Walt Disney, J. P. Morgan, and Merck were added to the average.

As far as bankruptcies, in its 100-year history the only company that has fallen off of the Dow Industrial Average due to financial difficulties is the John Manville company, which was caught in a wave of litigation relating to its premier fire-retardant product — asbestos. Chrysler's run-in with red ink that was eventually resolved by a bailout from the U.S. government was probably responsible for its deletion in the early 1980s, although the company never did, in fact, go bankrupt. The only other high-profile bankruptcy was Texaco, after the attempted acquisition of Getty Oil resulted in a major fine due to a breach of contract. Even Exxon's Valdez disaster and Union Carbide's Bhopal tragedy were just minor inconveniences by comparison.

Although these additions and deletions to the DJIA might appear to be only cosmetic, they have had an impact that few can fully appreciate without exhaustively researching the topic. For instance, in 1939 American Telephone & Telegraph (AT&T) was substituted for International Business Machines

(IBM). If this substitution had not been made, the Dow would have broken 1000 in 1961 instead of 1972, and would be considerably higher than it is today. IBM was only returned to the Dow in 1979, making one wonder if another milestone — the sacred 2000-point barrier — might have been penetrated in the mid-1970s instead of the mid-1980s if that substitution had not occurred.

Dow Mechanics

There are currently 30 stocks listed on the Dow Jones Industrial Average, 20 in the Dow Jones Transportation Average, and 15 in the Dow Jones Utility Average.

The precursor to the modern Dow Jones Industrial Average started with only 11 stocks in 1884, but has gradually grown to its current 30-stock roster over the past 100 years. There have been three big jumps: in 1896 the average was 12 stocks; 1916 saw the expansion of the average from 12 to 20 stocks; and, in 1928, the final move from 20 to 30 stocks was made. Although it is easy to find out what companies are currently on the various Dow Averages, the actual mechanics for computing the averages are much less transparent.

When Dow created his first eleven-stock average, he simply divided the total of all the prices by eleven (the number of stocks in the average) to get his result. Living in the days before frequent stock splits and stock dividends, Dow did not foresee events that would make the divisor change. As markets matured, companies began to use stock splits to try to keep the price of their shares within certain parameters. Until the implementation of the "Dow Divisor," Dow Jones would account for splits by multiplying the stock price by the number of shares into which each share was split. Unless it did this, a two-for-one split in one of the stocks would have caused a significant drop in the average that was not the result of any fundamental change. For example, if General Electric had split two-for-one at some point in the past, one would multiply the current price of General Electric by two before figuring out the Dow average.

Under this policy, the DJIA simply reflected the results of what a simple buy-and-hold strategy would have attained — neutralizing the effects of stock splits. However, stocks that split their shares numerous times would come to have more and more power over the daily moves of the Dow, because their small daily movements would be multiplied to account for numerous splits. This distorted the average by making it "split-weighted" (allowing companies that split their shares more frequently to have a disproportionate control over the average). To correct this, the editors of Dow Jones developed the Dow Divisor — a single number that took splits for each individual stock into account.

The Dow was first computed using the Dow Divisor on September 10, 1928. Norman Fosback describes how the Dow Divisor works in his book *Stock Market Logic:*

"Assume that the prices of the 30 stocks summed to $3,000. Then the 30-stock average price would be $3,000 divided by 30, or 100.00. If one of the 30 stocks was quoted at $200, but then split two-for-one so that its price fell to $100, the sum of prices would be only $2,900. To maintain the Average at its actual level of 100.00, the divisor of the Average is systematically altered. Since $2,900 divided by 100.00 equals 29, the new divisor is set at 29, down from 30, in effect preserving the average price at $100 ($2,900 divided by 29 still equals 100.00)."

Dow Jones currently adjusts the Dow Divisor if any event affects the Dow Jones Industrial Average by 5.0 or more points. Stock splits are not the only force that impacts the Dow Jones Industrial Average — stock dividends have an effect as well. When a stock pays a dividend, the "specialist" who facilitates trades in the stock at the exchange deducts the amount of the dividend, rounded to the nearest 1/8th, from the price of the stock. For example, if General Electric was trading at $50 and was scheduled to pay a $1 quarterly dividend on June 1st, General Electric would trade "ex-dividend" on June 2nd at only $49 a share and shareholders of General Electric would have the stock ($49) and the dividend ($1), for a total of $50 worth of stock and dividends. Large one-time cash or stock dividends and spin-offs of subsidiaries can move the average a lot more than 5.0 points, so the Divisor is constantly being adjusted to account for all of this.

This Divisor approach worked well for the first few decades, but in recent years the Divisor has started to become very small. In 1986, the Dow Divisor fell below 1.0 for the first time — effectively becoming the "Dow Multiplier," since to divide by a fraction, you invert it and multiply (resulting in a larger number).

With the Dow Divisor for the Industrials at about 0.346 as of this writing, the prices of the stocks on the average are effectively tripled when the Dow is computed. This creates a situation where even a fractional movement in the price of the Dow Industrial stocks (say up or down by a half-point) results in relatively large movements in the average.

If by some chance more than a few of the Dow Industrials trade ex-dividend on the same day, the difference between the last evening's close and that morning's open can be as much as 20 points. Since all of the 30 stocks currently pay dividends, this happens more frequently than most would imagine. Anyone interested in looking up the current Dow Divisor for the Industrials or any other Dow average can find the information every day in *The Wall Street Journal's* "Money and Investing" section in the "Dow Jones Averages" area.

As a result of the way the Dow is computed, the average has effectively become a "price-weighted" measure of the market. The Divisor simply measures the sum of the day's changes — there is nothing in it to account for the fact that a $1 change in a $15 stock is, percentage-wise, greater than a $1 change in a $100 stock. Because it measures all net changes in the same way, in effect it is a weighting system that tilts movements in the average toward the higher-priced stocks. A $1 move up or down in a $100 stock is a commonplace event, whereas a $1 change in a $15 stock is rarer.

The Divisor does not correct for the relative scarcity of the large changes in "value" represented by a $1 move in a $15 stock. The higher-priced stocks affect the average more since they are prone to make more $1 movements, even though, on a percentage or valuation basis, these moves are smaller than an equivalent $1 move in a $10 stock. Although this might make one question whether the DJIA is truly representative of the New York Stock Exchange (the original intent) or the broader market (its de facto contemporary function), it helps us better understand the day-to-day movements in the Dow Jones Industrial Average. ◆

FURTHER RESEARCH

By the time you read this, it's very possible that we'll be in the midst of discussing new developments in the history of the Dow Approach in the Motley Fool online. Research there doesn't ever really stop. That's the nature of a group project-ongoing education. And if we've learned nothing else in the first few years of The Motley Fool, we've learned that the Fool is like an enormous investment club, with the combined energies of the participants equaling more than the sum of all the parts. In addition, we are always updating and improving the online areas.

So visit us online and join in the ongoing process of discovery in the Dow Dividend Approach/Foolish Four area on The Motley Fool at www.fool.com, or at keyword Fool on America Online.

The Motley Fool also offers a spreadsheet that includes all the stocks on the Dow Jones Industrial Average and their annual returns — from 1961 through the last full year (nearly four decades!). The Dow Dividend Approach spreadsheet offers 37 years (1961–1997) of Dow stock information, with individual returns and dividends for each Dow stock as well as average annual and total returns for several major Dow Dividend Approach variations. Everything from stock dividends to spin-offs is exhaustively accounted for. If you're interested in this product, head over to our online store FoolMart (http://www.foolmart.com) or call 1-888-665-FOOL.

FINAL THOUGHTS

Having read this Foolish guide to the Dow Dividend Approach, you now know about three simple methods that have wildly outperformed the market for the past 35 years. But we didn't promise you mere outperformance, we promised you would *crush* your mutual funds. According to data from Morningstar, over the last 10 years the Foolish Four's average annual return out-performed 98% of all mutual funds. The RP4 variation outperformed all but 5 — that's not 5%, that's 5 out of the 1514 funds that Morningstar tracks. To put it another way, the RP4 beat 1509 out of the 1514 mutual funds that have been in business for 10 or more years. Even the super-safe High-Yield Ten has beaten the market (which beats over 90% of all mutual funds). The High-Yield Ten, Foolish Four, and RP4 variations have backhanded the stock market's average return and left it and the mutual fund industry — like a speedboat disappearing into the sun streaked horizon — far in its wake.

Whatever you do, invest with confidence. Investing in stocks is an exciting but sometimes harrowing experience, and volatility in stock prices is to be expected — but don't allow yourself to get thrown from your horse. Only invest in stocks if you're certain that you have a long-term outlook (at least 5 to 10 years) and then stick to your conviction and remind yourself that stocks outperform all other investment vehicles over the long term. In the near term, anything can happen in the stock market, but with these simple strategies you're investing in an easy and effective Foolish approach that has performed well in both good times and bad. Although these strategies have experienced down years, too, they have performed incredibly well over the long term for those who have stuck with them.

Fool on! ◆

Appendix

TABLE OF CONTENTS

Appendix A

COMPONENT STOCKS OF THE DOW

COMPONENT STOCKS OF THE DOW

AT&T Corporation (T)
32 Avenue of the Americas
New York, NY 10013
212-387-5400
http://www.att.com

AlliedSignal Inc. (ALD)
101 Columbia Rd.
Morristown, NJ 07962-1057
973-455-2000
http://www.alliedsignal.com

Aluminum Company of America (AA)
Alcoa Bldg., 425 6th Ave.
Pittsburgh, PA 15219-1850
412-553-4545
http://www.alcoa.com

American Express Company (AXP)
World Financial Center,
200 Vesey St.
New York, NY 10285
212-640-2000
http://www.americanexpress.com

The Boeing Company (BA)
7755 E. Marginal Way South
Seattle, WA 98108
206-655-2121
http://www.boeing.com

Caterpillar Inc. (CAT)
100 NE Adams St.
Peoria, IL 61629
309-675-1000
http://www.caterpillar.com

Chevron Corp. (CHV)
575 Market St.
San Francisco, CA 94105
415-894-7700
http://www.chevron.com

Citigroup (CCI)
153 E. 53rd St.
New York, NY 10043
800-285-3000
http://www.citigroup.com

Coca-Cola Co. (KO)
One Coca-Cola Plaza
Atlanta, GA 30313
404-676-2121
http://www.cocacola.com

Walt Disney Co. (DIS)
500 S. Buena Vista St.
Burbank, CA 91521
818-560-1000
http://www.disney.com

E. I. DuPont de Nemours & Co. (DD)
1007 Market St.
Wilmington, DE 19898
302-774-1000
http://www.dupont.com

Eastman Kodak Co. (EK)
343 State St.
Rochester, NY 14650
716-724-4000
http://www.kodak.com

EXXON CORP. (XON)
5959 Las Colinas Blvd.
Irving, TX 75039-2298
972-444-1000
http://www.exxon.com

GENERAL ELECTRIC CO. (GE)
3135 Easton Tpke.
Fairfield, CT 06431-0001
203-373-2211
http://www.ge.com

GENERAL MOTORS CORP. (GM)
100 Renaissance Center
Detroit, MI 48243-7301
313-556-5000
http://www.gm.com

GOODYEAR TIRE & RUBBER CO. (GT)
1144 E. Market St.
Akron, OH 44316-0001
330-796-2121
http://www.goodyear.com

HEWLETT-PACKARD CO. (HWP)
3000 Hanover St.
Palo Alto, CA 94304
650-857-1501
http://www.hp.com

INTERNATIONAL BUSINESS MACHINES CORP. (IBM)
New Orchard Rd.
Armonk, NY 10504
914-765-1900
http://www.ibm.com

INTERNATIONAL PAPER CO. (IP)
2 Manhattanville Rd.
Purchase, NY 10577
914-397-1500
http://www.ipaper.com

JOHNSON & JOHNSON (JNJ)
One Johnson & Johnson Plaza
New Brunswick, NJ 08933
732-524-0400
http://www.jnj.com

McDONALD'S CORP. (MCD)
McDonald's Plaza
Oak Brook, IL 60523
630-623-3000
http://www.mcdonalds.com

MERCK & CO., INC. (MRK)
1 Merck Dr.
Whitehouse Station, NJ 08889-0100
908-423-1000
http://www.merck.com

MINNESOTA MINING & MANUFACTURING CO. (MMM)
3M Center
St. Paul, MN 55144-1000
651-733-1110
http://www.mmm.com

J. P. MORGAN & CO. (JPM)
60 Wall St.
New York, NY 10260-0060
212-483-2323
http://www.jpmorgan.com

PHILIP MORRIS COS. (MO)
120 Park Ave.
New York, NY 10017
212-880-5000
http://nt1.irin.com/irin/Detail.CFM/mo

PROCTER & GAMBLE CO. (PG)
One Procter & Gamble Plaza
Cincinnati, OH 45202
513-983-1100
http://www.pg.com

SEARS, ROEBUCK & CO. (S)
3333 Beverly Rd.
Hoffman Estates, IL 60179
847-286-2500
http://www.sears.com

UNION CARBIDE CORP. (UK)
39 Old Ridgebury Rd.
Danbury, CT 06817-0001
203-794-2000
http://www.unioncarbide.com

UNITED TECHNOLOGIES CORP. (UTX)
One Financial Plaza
Hartford, CT 06101
860-728-7000
http://www.utc.com

WAL-MART STORES INC. (WMT)
702 SW 8th St.
Bentonville, AR 72716-8611
501-273-4000
http://www.wal-mart.com

Appendix

B

HISTORICAL RETURNS OF THE THREE VARIATIONS

HISTORICAL RETURNS
OF THE THREE VARIATIONS

Average Annual Returns by Year

Annual Returns

Year	High-Yield 10	Foolish Four	RP4	S&P500	Dow 30
1963	21.06%	17.42%	18.62%	22.80%	22.98%
1964	20.28%	26.79%	24.66%	16.48%	17.94%
1965	19.34%	12.40%	15.84%	12.45%	17.31%
1966	-17.90%	-17.65%	-22.89%	-10.06%	-15.08%
1967	25.68%	40.91%	34.07%	23.98%	21.75%
1968	14.68%	14.09%	18.34%	11.06%	10.11%
1969	-12.77%	-6.66%	-8.41%	-8.50%	-9.27%
1970	4.73%	-5.92%	-14.20%	4.01%	5.04%
1971	5.71%	19.74%	19.74%	14.31%	9.10%
1972	23.79%	24.91%	16.59%	18.98%	16.69%
1973	3.89%	25.74%	17.28%	-14.66%	-10.86%
1974	1.04%	5.25%	20.00%	-26.47%	-15.64%
1975	52.17%	68.71%	68.71%	37.20%	44.25%
1976	33.24%	36.92%	37.93%	23.84%	29.36%
1977	1.17%	5.32%	-2.96%	-7.18%	-12.58%
1978	2.44%	9.89%	9.89%	6.56%	2.53%
1979	9.69%	2.17%	17.70%	18.44%	11.34%
1980	32.95%	48.18%	24.20%	32.42%	25.29%
1981	4.87%	-4.63%	9.66%	-4.91%	-3.30%
1982	20.87%	41.58%	56.88%	21.41%	19.80%
1983	38.43%	41.74%	36.72%	22.51%	35.35%
1984	7.45%	10.24%	10.30%	6.27%	-0.12%
1985	30.61%	22.85%	49.82%	32.16%	30.98%
1986	29.43%	27.30%	29.67%	18.47%	21.87%
1987	8.56%	18.75%	17.89%	5.23%	15.93%
1988	17.96%	13.62%	22.08%	16.81%	13.78%
1989	29.64%	15.28%	47.35%	31.49%	31.95%
1990	-10.01%	-17.61%	-17.61%	-3.17%	-9.14%
1991	35.24%	81.61%	34.81%	30.55%	30.36%
1992	6.35%	29.94%	29.94%	7.67%	11.00%
1993	23.54%	26.22%	30.26%	9.99%	17.91%
1994	2.43%	4.72%	7.59%	1.31%	3.73%
1995	37.10%	30.42%	47.05%	37.43%	36.69%
1996	27.47%	24.34%	26.56%	23.07%	24.32%
1997	20.39%	22.31%	19.49%	33.36%	22.33%

35-Year Compound Average Annual Returns (1963–1997)

	High-Yield 10	Foolish Four	RP4	S&P500	Dow 30
1963–1997	15.26%	18.74%	19.84%	12.16%	12.41%

25-Year Compound Average Annual Returns (1973–1997)

	High-Yield 10	Foolish Four	RP4	S&P500	Dow 30
1973–1997	17.69%	21.86%	24.62%	13.06%	13.83%

Returns do not include taxes or commissions. All variations include reinvested dividends. Each portfolio is rebalanced annually on the first trading day of the year to invest in equal dollar amounts of each stock. The Dow 30 portfolio returns will be slightly different from the returns on the Dow Jones Industrial Average (DJIA) index since index returns are based on an equal number of shares rather than equal dollar amounts in each stock.

Appendix C

YEARLY RETURNS FOR THE COMPONENT STOCKS OF EACH APPROACH

YEARLY RETURNS FOR THE COMPONENT STOCKS OF EACH APPROACH

1963

Company	Tkr	Return	High Yield Rank	Low Price Rank	RP Rank
High-Yield 10					
Bethlehem Steel	BS	+17.24%	*1*	2	1
American Tobacco	AT	+1.28%	*2*	3	2
Anaconda Co.	A	+23.17%	*3*	4	4
International Harvester	HR	+22.36%	*4*		7
Johns Manville	JM	+22.02%	*5*	5	5
US Steel	X	+30.00%	*6*		6
American Can	AC	+0.55%	*7*		9
Allied Chemical	ACD	+31.91%	*8*		10
Standard Oil, New Jersey	J	+34.12%	*9*		13
International Paper	IP	+27.99%	*10*	1	3
Total Average Return		**+21.06%**			

Company	Tkr	Return	High Yield Rank	Low Price Rank	RP Rank
Foolish Four					
International Paper	IP	+27.99%	10	*1*	3
Bethlehem Steel	BS	+17.24%	1	*2*	1
American Tobacco	AT	+1.28%	2	*3*	2
Anaconda Co.	A	+23.17%	3	*4*	4
Total Average Return		**+17.42%**			

Company	Tkr	Return	High Yield Rank	Low Price Rank	RP Rank
RP4					
American Tobacco	AT	+1.28%	2	3	*2*
International Paper	IP	+27.99%	10	1	*3*
Anaconda Co.	A	+23.17%	3	4	*4*
Johns Manville	JM	+22.02%	5	5	*5*
Total Average Return		**+18.62%**			

Total Average Return of S&P 500	**+22.80%**
Total Average Return of Dow 30	**+22.98%**

1964

Company	Tkr	Return	High Yield Rank	Low Price Rank	RP Rank
High-Yield 10					
American Tobacco	AT	+26.13%	*1*	1	1
United Aircraft	UA	+54.07%	*2*	3	3
Bethlehem Steel	BS	+12.31%	*3*	2	2
American Can	AC	+3.71%	*4*	4	4
Anaconda Co.	A	+14.32%	*5*		6
International Harvester	HR	+31.22%	*6*		10
Johns Manville	JM	+12.69%	*7*		7
Woolworth	Z	+15.13%	*8*		13
Swift	SWX	+37.09%	*9*	4	9
US Steel	X	-3.87%	*10*		11
Total Average Return		**+20.28%**			
Foolish Four					
Bethlehem Steel	BS	+12.31%	3	*2*	2
United Aircraft	UA	+54.07%	2	*3*	3
American Can	AC	+3.71%	4	*4*	4
Swift	SWX	+37.09%	9	*4*	9
Total Average Return		**+26.79%**			
RP4					
Bethlehem Steel	BS	+12.31%	3	2	*2*
United Aircraft	UA	+54.07%	2	3	*3*
American Can	AC	+3.71%	4	4	*4*
Westinghouse Electric	WX	+28.53%			*5*
Total Average Return		**+24.66%**			

Total Average Return of S&P 500   **+16.48%**
Total Average Return of Dow 30   **+17.94%**

1965

Company	Tkr	Return	High Yield Rank	Low Price Rank	RP Rank
High-Yield 10					
American Tobacco	AT	+18.52%	*1*	3	1
American Can	AC	+32.28%	*2*	5	3
Bethlehem Steel	BS	+18.21%	*3*	4	2
US Steel	X	+6.16%	*4*		6
Anaconda Co.	A	+67.78%	*5*		7
International Harvester	HR	+27.49%	*6*		11
Johns Manville	JM	+7.80%	*7*		8
International Paper	IP	-3.42%	*8*	2	5
Woolworth	Z	+16.29%	*9*	1	4
Allied Chemical	ACD	+2.28%	*10*		9
Total Average Return		**+19.34%**			
Foolish Four					
Woolworth	Z	+16.29%	9	*1*	4
International Paper	IP	-3.42%	8	*2*	5
American Tobacco	AT	+18.52%	1	*3*	1
Bethlehem Steel	BS	+18.21%	3	*4*	2
Total Average Return		**+12.40%**			
RP4					
Bethlehem Steel	BS	+18.21%	3	4	*2*
American Can	AC	+32.28%	2	5	*3*
Woolworth	Z	+16.29%	9	1	*4*
International Paper	IP	-3.42%	8	2	*5*
Total Average Return		**+15.84%**			

Total Average Return of S&P 500 +12.45%
Total Average Return of Dow 30 +17.31%

1966

Company	Tkr	Return	High Yield Rank	Low Price Rank	RP Rank
High-Yield 10					
Standard Oil, New Jersey	J	-17.43%	1		10
American Tobacco	AT	-12.86%	2	2	2
Johns Manville	JM	-9.53%	3		7
International Paper	IP	-12.75%	4	1	1
Allied Chemical	ACD	-25.67%	5	4	5
US Steel	X	-21.73%	6	5	6
Bethlehem Steel	BS	-19.31%	7	3	3
Swift	SWX	-10.98%	8		8
Chrysler	C	-38.28%	9		9
American Can	AC	-10.47%	10		11
Total Average Return		**-17.90%**			
Foolish Four					
International Paper	IP	-12.75%	4	1	1
American Tobacco	AT	-12.86%	2	2	2
Bethlehem Steel	BS	-19.31%	7	3	3
Allied Chemical	ACD	-25.67%	5	4	5
Total Average Return		**-17.65%**			
RP4					
American Tobacco	AT	-12.86%	2	2	2
Bethlehem Steel	BS	-19.31%	7	3	3
Woolworth	Z	-33.73%			4
Allied Chemical	ACD	-25.67%	5	4	5
Total Average Return		**-22.89%**			

Total Average Return of S&P 500   **-10.06%**
Total Average Return of Dow 30   **-15.08%**

1967

Company	Tkr	Return	High Yield Rank	Low Price Rank	RP Rank
High-Yield 10					
Anaconda Co.	A	+22.98%	*1*		6
Chrysler	C	+86.40%	*2*	4	2
US Steel	X	+15.65%	*3*		5
American Tobacco	AT	+7.24%	*4*	5	4
Allied Chemical	ACD	+25.68%	*5*		7
International Paper	IP	+27.00%	*6*	2	3
International Harvester	HR	+7.31%	*7*		9
Woolworth	Z	+35.03%	*8*	1	1
Standard Oil, New Jersey	J	+14.32%	*9*		13
Bethlehem Steel	BS	+15.23%	*10*	3	8
Total Average Return		**+25.68%**			
Foolish Four					
Woolworth	Z	+35.03%	8	*1*	1
International Paper	IP	+27.00%	6	*2*	3
Bethlehem Steel	BS	+15.23%	10	*3*	8
Chrysler	C	+86.40%	2	*4*	2
Total Average Return		**+40.91%**			
RP4					
Chrysler	C	+86.40%	2	4	*2*
International Paper	IP	+27.00%	6	2	*3*
American Tobacco	AT	+7.24%	4	5	*4*
US Steel	X	+15.65%	3		*5*
Total Average Return		**+34.07%**			

Total Average Return of S&P 500   +23.98%
Total Average Return of Dow 30   +21.75%

1968

Company	Tkr	Return	High Yield Rank	Low Price Rank	RP Rank
High-Yield 10					
Standard Oil, New Jersey	J	+19.42%	1		9
US Steel	X	+8.96%	2		2
American Tobacco	AT	+26.74%	3	2	1
Anaconda Co.	A	+40.58%	4		7
International Harvester	HR	+9.26%	5	4	3
Allied Chemical	ACD	-3.19%	6	5	8
American Telephone and Telegraph	T	+8.28%	7		11
Bethlehem Steel	BS	-1.94%	8	3	6
International Paper	IP	+22.31%	9	1	4
American Can	AC	+16.37%	10		12
Total Average Return		**+14.68%**			
Foolish Four					
International Paper	IP	+22.31%	9	1	4
American Tobacco	AT	+26.74%	3	2	1
Bethlehem Steel	BS	-1.94%	8	3	6
International Harvester	HR	+9.26%	5	4	3
Total Average Return		**+14.09%**			
RP4					
US Steel	X	+8.96%	2		2
International Harvester	HR	+9.26%	5	4	3
International Paper	IP	+22.31%	9	1	4
Woolworth	Z	+32.84%			5
Total Average Return		**+18.34%**			

Total Average Return of S&P 500   +11.06%
Total Average Return of Dow 30   +10.11%

1969

Company	Tkr	Return	High Yield Rank	Low Price Rank	RP Rank
High-Yield 10					
US Steel	X	-14.60%	*1*	5	2
Standard Oil, New Jersey	J	-16.51%	*2*		8
Bethlehem Steel	BS	-7.60%	*3*	1	1
American Brands	AMB	-3.53%	*4*	4	4
International Harvester	HR	-24.78%	*5*	3	3
American Telephone and Telegraph	T	-3.13%	*6*		7
Union Carbide	UK	-12.57%	*7*		6
General Motors	GM	-5.71%	*8*		14
International Paper	IP	+9.28%	*9*	2	5
Anaconda Co.	A	-48.52%	*10*		12
Total Average Return		**-12.77%**			

Company	Tkr	Return	High Yield Rank	Low Price Rank	RP Rank
Foolish Four					
Bethlehem Steel	BS	-7.60%	3	*1*	1
International Paper	IP	+9.28%	9	*2*	5
International Harvester	HR	-24.78%	5	*3*	3
American Brands	AMB	-3.53%	4	*4*	4
Total Average Return		**-6.66%**			

Company	Tkr	Return	High Yield Rank	Low Price Rank	RP Rank
RP4					
US Steel	X	-14.60%	1	5	*2*
International Harvester	HR	-24.78%	5	3	*3*
American Brands	AMB	-3.53%	4	4	*4*
International Paper	IP	+9.28%	9	2	*5*
Total Average Return		**-8.41%**			

Total Average Return of S&P 500	**-8.50%**
Total Average Return of Dow 30	**-9.27%**

1970

Company	Tkr	Return	High Yield Rank	Low Price Rank	RP Rank
High-Yield 10					
US Steel	X	-0.29%	*1*	4	3
International Harvester	HR	+12.15%	*2*	1	1
Standard Oil, New Jersey	J	+23.51%	*3*		9
Bethlehem Steel	BS	-10.41%	*4*	2	2
Anaconda Co.	A	-25.12%	*5*	3	4
Chrysler	C	-20.99%	*6*	5	5
American Brands	AMB	+32.56%	*7*		7
DuPont	DD	+27.65%	*8*		18
Standard Oil, California	SD	+7.75%	*9*		13
American Can	AC	+0.48%	*10*		11
Total Average Return		**+4.73%**			

Company	Tkr	Return	High Yield Rank	Low Price Rank	RP Rank
Foolish Four					
International Harvester	HR	+12.15%	2	*1*	1
Bethlehem Steel	BS	-10.41%	4	*2*	2
Anaconda Co.	A	-25.12%	5	*3*	4
US Steel	X	-0.29%	1	*4*	3
Total Average Return		**-5.92%**			

Company	Tkr	Return	High Yield Rank	Low Price Rank	RP Rank
RP4					
Bethlehem Steel	BS	-10.41%	4	2	*2*
US Steel	X	-0.29%	1	4	*3*
Anaconda Co.	A	-25.12%	5	3	*4*
Chrysler	C	-20.99%	6	5	*5*
Total Average Return		**-14.20%**			

Total Average Return of S&P 500   +4.01%
Total Average Return of Dow 30   +5.04%

1971

Company	Tkr	Return	High Yield Rank	Low Price Rank	RP Rank
High-Yield 10					
Anaconda Co.	A	-21.89%	*1*	1	1
Bethlehem Steel	BS	+35.33%	*2*	2	2
US Steel	X	+0.78%	*3*	5	3
International Harvester	HR	+13.64%	*4*	4	4
Standard Oil, New Jersey	J	+5.75%	*5*		14
American Can	AC	-8.30%	*6*		7
United Aircraft	UA	-7.66%	*7*		6
American Telephone and Telegraph	T	-2.87%	*8*		10
Standard Oil, California	SD	+13.18%	*9*		12
Allied Chemical	ACD	+29.20%	*10*	3	5
Total Average Return		**+5.71%**			
Foolish Four					
Bethlehem Steel	BS	+35.33%	2	*2*	2
Allied Chemical	ACD	+29.20%	10	*3*	5
International Harvester	HR	+13.64%	4	*4*	4
US Steel	X	+0.78%	3	*5*	3
Total Average Return		**+19.74%**			
RP4					
Bethlehem Steel	BS	+35.33%	2	2	*2*
US Steel	X	+0.78%	3	5	*3*
International Harvester	HR	+13.64%	4	4	*4*
Allied Chemical	ACD	+29.20%	10	3	*5*
Total Average Return		**+19.74%**			

Total Average Return of S&P 500   +14.31%
Total Average Return of Dow 30   +9.10%

1972

Company	Tkr	Return	High Yield Rank	Low Price Rank	RP Rank
High-Yield 10					
American Can	AC	-1.24%	*1*	4	2
United Aircraft	UA	+58.29%	*2*	1	1
American Telephone and Telegraph	T	+25.03%	*3*		4
Exxon	XON	+25.75%	*4*		12
US Steel	X	+7.30%	*5*	3	3
American Brands	AMB	+7.51%	*6*		6
Standard Oil, California	SD	+43.77%	*7*		14
International Harvester	HR	+35.29%	*8*	2	5
Union Carbide	UK	+24.93%	*9*		11
Texaco, Inc.	TX	+11.25%	*10*	5	7
Total Average Return		**+23.79%**			
Foolish Four					
United Aircraft	UA	+58.29%	2	*1*	1
International Harvester	HR	+35.29%	8	*2*	5
US Steel	X	+7.30%	5	*3*	3
American Can	AC	-1.24%	1	*4*	2
Total Average Return		**+24.91%**			
RP4					
American Can	AC	-1.24%	1	4	*2*
US Steel	X	+7.30%	5	3	*3*
American Telephone and Telegraph	T	+25.03%	3		*4*
International Harvester	HR	+35.29%	8	2	*5*
Total Average Return		**+16.59%**			

Total Average Return of S&P 500	**+18.98%**
Total Average Return of Dow 30	**+16.69%**

1973

Company	Tkr	Return	High Yield Rank	Low Price Rank	RP Rank
High-Yield 10					
American Can	AC	-8.06%	*1*	5	1
American Brands	AMB	-16.56%	*2*		4
American Telephone and Telegraph	T	-0.71%	*3*		8
US Steel	X	+24.82%	*4*	4	2
General Foods	GF	-9.74%	*5*	1	3
Texaco, Inc.	TX	-15.59%	*6*		7
Exxon Corp	XON	+14.49%	*7*		19
General Motors	GM	-37.60%	*8*		20
Allied Chemical	ACD	+71.63%	*9*	2	5
Bethlehem Steel	BS	+16.26%	*9*	2	5
Total Average Return		**+3.89%**			

Company	Tkr	Return	High Yield Rank	Low Price Rank	RP Rank
Foolish Four					
General Foods	GF	-9.74%	5	*1*	3
Allied Chemical	ACD	+71.63%	9	*2*	5
Bethlehem Steel	BS	+16.26%	9	*2*	5
US Steel	X	+24.82%	4	*4*	2
Total Average Return		**+25.74%**			

Company	Tkr	Return	High Yield Rank	Low Price Rank	RP Rank
RP4					
US Steel	X	+24.82%	4	4	*2*
General Foods	GF	-9.74%	5	1	*3*
American Brands	AMB	-16.56%	2		*4*
Allied Chemical*	ACD	+71.63%	9	2	*5**
Bethlehem Steel*	BS	+16.26%	9	2	*5**
Total Average Return		**+17.28%**			

*These two stocks tied for 5th place so both were included. For 1973 only, the RP4 held 5 stocks.

Total Average Return of S&P 500	**-14.66%**
Total Average Return of Dow 30	**-10.86%**

1974

Company	Tkr	Return	High Yield Rank	Low Price Rank	RP Rank
High-Yield 10					
Chrysler	C	-37.85%	*1*	1	1
American Can	AC	+18.88%	*2*		4
United Aircraft	UA	+42.95%	*3*	5	5
General Motors	GM	-23.32%	*4*		10
Johns Manville	JM	+26.02%	*5*	3	2
American Brands	AMB	+1.67%	*6*		7
Woolworth	Z	-40.14%	*7*	4	6
Goodyear Tire and Rubber	GT	-7.84%	*8*	2	3
Union Carbide	UK	+31.51%	*9*		12
American Telephone and Telegraph	T	-1.52%	*10*		13
Total Average Return		**+1.04%**			
Foolish Four					
Goodyear Tire and Rubber	GT	-7.84%	8	*2*	3
Johns Manville	JM	+26.02%	5	*3*	2
Woolworth	Z	-40.14%	7	*4*	6
United Aircraft	UA	+42.95%	3	*5*	5
Total Average Return		**+5.25%**			
RP4					
Johns Manville	JM	+26.02%	5	3	*2*
Goodyear Tire and Rubber	GT	-7.84%	8	2	*3*
American Can	AC	+18.88%	2		*4*
United Aircraft	UA	+42.95%	3	5	*5*
Total Average Return		**+20.00%**			

Total Average Return of S&P 500   -26.47%
Total Average Return of Dow 30   -15.64%

1975

Company	Tkr	Return	High Yield Rank	Low Price Rank	RP Rank
High-Yield 10					
Chrysler	C	+40.63%	*1*	1	1
Woolworth	Z	+136.20%	*2*	2	2
General Motors	GM	+90.67%	*3*		7
Westinghouse Electric	WX	+41.70%	*4*	3	3
Exxon Corp	XON	+43.40%	*5*		16
Texaco, Inc.	TX	+16.29%	*6*		6
Standard Oil, California	SD	+33.33%	*7*		9
International Harvester	HR	+22.59%	*8*		8
Anaconda Co.	A	+23.28%	*9*	5	5
Goodyear Tire and Rubber	GT	+73.64%	*10*	4	4
Total Average Return		**+52.17%**			
Foolish Four					
Woolworth	Z	+136.20%	2	*2*	2
Westinghouse Electric	WX	+41.70%	4	*3*	3
Goodyear Tire and Rubber	GT	+73.64%	10	*4*	4
Anaconda Co.	A	+23.28%	9	*5*	5
Total Average Return		**+68.71**			
RP4					
Woolworth	Z	+136.20%	2	2	*2*
Westinghouse Electric	WX	+41.70%	4	3	*3*
Goodyear Tire and Rubber	GT	+73.64%	10	4	*4*
Anaconda Co.	A	+23.28%	9	5	*5*
Total Average Return		**+68.71%**			

Total Average Return of S&P 500   +37.20%
Total Average Return of Dow 30   +44.25%

1976

Company	Tkr	Return	High Yield Rank	Low Price Rank	RP Rank
High-Yield 10					
Texaco, Inc.	TX	+23.56%	*1*	3	2
International Harvester	HR	+49.68%	*2*	2	3
Westinghouse Electric	WX	+38.11%	*3*	1	1
American Can	AC	+33.47%	*4*		4
American Brands	AMB	+24.00%	*5*		7
Standard Oil, California	SD	+45.00%	*6*	5	5
American Telephone and Telegraph	T	+32.04%	*7*		13
Bethlehem Steel	BS	+25.00%	*8*		11
Exxon Corp	XON	+25.22%	*9*		18
International Nickel of Canada	N	+36.35%	*10*	4	8
Total Average Return		**+33.24%**			
Foolish Four					
Westinghouse Electric	WX	+38.11%	3	*1*	1
International Harvester	HR	+49.68%	2	*2*	3
Texaco, Inc.	TX	+23.56%	1	*3*	2
International Nickel of Canada	N	+36.35%	10	*4*	8
Total Average Return		**+36.92%**			
RP4					
Texaco, Inc.	TX	+23.56%	1	3	*2*
International Harvester	HR	+49.68%	2	2	*3*
American Can	AC	+33.47%	4		*4*
Standard Oil, California	SD	+45.00%	6	5	*5*
Total Average Return		**+37.93%**			

Total Average Return of S&P 500	**+23.84%**
Total Average Return of Dow 30	**+29.36%**

1977

Company	Tkr	Return	High Yield Rank	Low Price Rank	RP Rank
High-Yield 10					
Texaco, Inc.	TX	+7.27%	*1*	2	1
American Brands	AMB	+0.51%	*2*		7
American Can	AC	+5.62%	*3*		4
American Telephone and Telegraph	T	+1.30%	*4*		12
International Harvester	HR	-4.07%	*5*	4	3
Westinghouse Electric	WX	+8.41%	*6*	1	2
Standard Oil, California	SD	-0.68%	*7*		10
Exxon Corp	XON	-6.06%	*8*		16
Esmark Inc.	ESM	-10.25%	*9*	5	9
General Foods	GF	+9.67%	*10*	3	8
Total Average Return		**+1.17%**			
Foolish Four					
Westinghouse Electric	WX	+8.41%	6	*1*	2
Texaco, Inc.	TX	+7.27%	1	*2*	1
General Foods	GF	+9.67%	10	*3*	8
International Harvester	HR	-4.07%	5	*4*	3
Total Average Return		**+5.32%**			
RP4					
Westinghouse Electric	WX	+8.41%	6	1	*2*
International Harvester	HR	-4.07%	5	4	*3*
American Can	AC	+5.62%	3		*4*
Goodyear Tire and Rubber	GT	-21.79%			*5*
Total Average Return		**-2.96%**			

Total Average Return of S&P 500   -7.18%
Total Average Return of Dow 30   -12.58%

1978

Company	Tkr	Return	High Yield Rank	Low Price Rank	RP Rank
High-Yield 10					
Chrysler	C	-19.01%	*1*	1	1
Woolworth	Z	+12.30%	*2*	3	3
Goodyear Tire and Rubber	GT	+1.01%	*3*	2	2
Texaco, Inc.	TX	-5.45%	*4*	4	4
American Brands	AMB	+27.06%	*5*		10
International Harvester	HR	+31.73%	*6*	5	5
United States Steel	X	-24.38%	*7*		7
American Telephone and Telegraph	T	+8.92%	*8*		18
Union Carbide	UK	-7.00%	*9*		11
General Motors	GM	-0.81%	*10*		21
Total Average Return		**+2.44%**			

Company	Tkr	Return	High Yield Rank	Low Price Rank	RP Rank
Foolish Four					
Goodyear Tire and Rubber	GT	+1.01%	3	*2*	2
Woolworth	Z	+12.30%	2	*3*	3
Texaco, Inc.	TX	-5.45%	4	*4*	4
International Harvester	HR	+31.73%	6	*5*	5
Total Average Return		**+9.89%**			

Company	Tkr	Return	High Yield Rank	Low Price Rank	RP Rank
RP4					
Goodyear Tire and Rubber	GT	+1.01%	3	2	*2*
Woolworth	Z	+12.30%	2	3	*3*
Texaco, Inc.	TX	-5.45%	4	4	*4*
International Harvester	HR	+31.73%	6	5	*5*
Total Average Return		**+9.89%**			

Total Average Return of S&P 500	**+6.56%**
Total Average Return of Dow 30	**+2.53%**

1979

Company	Tkr	Return	High Yield Rank	Low Price Rank	RP Rank
High-Yield 10					
Texaco, Inc.	TX	+25.50%	*1*	3	2
Union Carbide	UK	+27.41%	*2*		10
Goodyear Tire and Rubber	GT	-12.77%	*3*	1	1
American Brands	AMB	+42.68%	*4*		15
American Telephone and Telegraph	T	-6.17%	*5*		20
Esmark Inc.	ESM	+19.86%	*6*	5	7
American Can	AC	+5.02%	*7*		12
Johns Manville	JM	+7.35%	*8*	3	6
General Motors	GM	-0.59%	*9*		18
United States Steel	X	-11.41%	*10*	2	5
Total Average Return		**+9.69%**			
Foolish Four					
Goodyear Tire and Rubber	GT	-12.77%	3	*1*	1
United States Steel	X	-11.41%	10	*2*	5
Texaco, Inc.	TX	+25.50%	1	*3*	2
Johns Manville	JM	+7.35%	8	*3*	6
Total Average Return		**+2.17%**			
RP4					
Texaco, Inc.	TX	+25.50%	1	3	*2*
Woolworth	Z	+33.81%			*3*
Owens Illinois	OI	+22.91%			*4*
United States Steel	X	-11.41%	10	2	*5*
Total Average Return		**+17.70%**			

Total Average Return of S&P 500   +18.44%
Total Average Return of Dow 30   +11.34%

1980

Company	Tkr	Return	High Yield Rank	Low Price Rank	RP Rank
High-Yield 10					
DuPont	DD	+12.93%	1		3
General Motors	GM	-1.62%	2		4
Goodyear Tire and Rubber	GT	+45.05%	3	1	1
Eastman Kodak	EK	+64.08%	4		9
American Telephone and Telegraph	T	+3.61%	5		12
United States Steel	X	+51.25%	6	2	2
Exxon Corp	XON	+60.60%	7		15
Johns Manville	JM	+12.23%	8	3	7
American Can	AC	-2.80%	9	5	11
Texaco, Inc.	TX	+84.20%	10	4	8
Total Average Return		**+32.95%**			
Foolish Four					
Goodyear Tire and Rubber	GT	+45.05%	3	1	1
United States Steel	X	+51.25%	6	2	2
Johns Manville	JM	+12.23%	8	3	7
Texaco, Inc.	TX	+84.20%	10	4	8
Total Average Return		**+48.18%**			
RP4					
United States Steel	X	+51.25%	6	2	2
DuPont	DD	+12.93%	1		3
General Motors	GM	-1.62%	2		4
Bethlehem Steel	BS	+34.22%			5
Total Average Return		**+24.20%**			

Total Average Return of S&P 500   +32.42%
Total Average Return of Dow 30   +25.29%

1981

Company	Tkr	Return	High Yield Rank	Low Price Rank	RP Rank
High-Yield 10					
American Telephone and Telegraph	T	+30.74%	1		5
American Can	AC	+24.27%	2		3
Sears, Roebuck	S	+17.65%	3	1	1
American Brands	AMB	+9.08%	4		12
Johns Manville	JM	-32.48%	5	3	4
Goodyear Tire and Rubber	GT	+16.12%	6	2	2
Exxon Corp	XON	-16.49%	7		17
General Foods	GF	+12.23%	8	5	7
Woolworth	Z	-19.80%	9	4	6
Eastman Kodak	EK	+7.37%	10		16
Total Average Return		**+4.87%**			
Foolish Four					
Sears, Roebuck	S	+17.65%	3	1	1
Goodyear Tire and Rubber	GT	+16.12%	6	2	2
Johns Manville	JM	-32.48%	5	3	4
Woolworth	Z	-19.80%	9	4	6
Total Average Return		**-4.63%**			
RP4					
Goodyear Tire and Rubber	GT	+16.12%	6	2	2
American Can	AC	+24.27%	2		3
Johns Manville	JM	-32.48%	5	3	4
American Telephone and Telegraph	T	+30.74%	1		5
Total Average Return		**+9.66%**			

Total Average Return of S&P 500   -4.91%
Total Average Return of Dow 30   -3.30%

1982

Company	Tkr	Return	High Yield Rank	Low Price Rank	RP Rank
High-Yield 10					
Manville Corp.	MAN	-21.48%	*1*	1	1
Woolworth	Z	+50.96%	*2*	3	2
Exxon Corp	XON	+3.64%	*3*	5	4
American Telephone and Telegraph	T	+11.58%	*4*		14
Texaco, Inc.	TX	+1.51%	*5*		6
American Brands	AMB	+25.24%	*6*		10
American Can	AC	-5.54%	*7*		9
Sears, Roebuck	S	+81.39%	*8*	2	3
Aluminum Company of America	AA	+30.31%	*9*	4	7
General Foods	GF	+31.10%	*10*		12
Total Average Return		**+20.87**			
Foolish Four					
Sears, Roebuck	S	+81.39%	8	*2*	3
Woolworth	Z	+50.96%	2	*3*	2
Aluminum Company of America	AA	+30.31%	9	*4*	7
Exxon Corp	XON	+3.64%	3	*5*	4
Total Average Return		**+41.58%**			
RP4					
Woolworth	Z	+50.96%	2	3	*2*
Sears, Roebuck	S	+81.39%	8	2	*3*
Exxon Corp	XON	+3.64%	3	5	*4*
Goodyear Tire and Rubber	GT	+91.52%			*5*
Total Average Return		**+56.88%**			

Total Average Return of S&P 500	**+21.41%**
Total Average Return of Dow 30	**+19.80%**

1983

Company	Tkr	Return	High Yield Rank	Low Price Rank	RP Rank
High-Yield 10					
Exxon Corp	XON	+36.98%	*1*	2	1
Texaco, Inc.	TX	+24.90%	*2*	3	2
American Can	AC	+60.24%	*3*	4	3
American Telephone and Telegraph	T	+14.15%	*4*		7
American Brands	AMB	+38.30%	*5*		8
Standard Oil, California	SD	+16.88%	*6*	5	5
Allied Corp.	ALD	+78.54%	*7*		6
Woolworth	Z	+44.85%	*8*	1	4
Union Carbide	UK	+27.54%	*9*		14
DuPont	DD	+41.91%	*10*		12
Total Average Return		**+38.43%**			
Foolish Four					
Woolworth	Z	+44.85%	8	*1*	4
Exxon Corp	XON	+36.98%	1	*2*	1
Texaco, Inc.	TX	+24.90%	2	*3*	2
American Can	AC	+60.24%	3	*4*	3
Total Average Return		**+41.74%**			
RP4					
Texaco, Inc.	TX	+24.90%	2	3	*2*
American Can	AC	+60.24%	3	4	*3*
Woolworth	Z	+44.85%	8	1	*4*
Standard Oil, California	SD	+16.88%	6	5	*5*
Total Average Return		**+36.72%**			
Total Average Return of S&P 500		**+22.51%**			
Total Average Return of Dow 30		**+35.35%**			

1984

Company	Tkr	Return	High Yield Rank	Low Price Rank	RP Rank
High-Yield 10					
Exxon Corp	XON	+30.65%	1	4	1
American Telephone and Telegraph	T	+26.13%	2		4
Texaco, Inc.	TX	+4.96%	3	2	2
Standard Oil, California	SD	-3.96%	4	1	3
American Can	AC	+14.07%	5	5	5
American Brands	AMB	+13.62%	6		8
Union Carbide	UK	-34.97%	7		12
DuPont	DD	+0.78%	8		9
General Motors	GM	+13.95%	9		15
Woolworth	Z	+9.30%	10	3	6
Total Average Return		**+7.45%**			

Company	Tkr	Return	High Yield Rank	Low Price Rank	RP Rank
Foolish Four					
Standard Oil, California	SD	-3.96%	4	1	3
Texaco, Inc.	TX	+4.96%	3	2	2
Woolworth	Z	+9.30%	10	3	6
Exxon Corp	XON	+30.65%	1	4	1
Total Average Return		**+10.24%**			

Company	Tkr	Return	High Yield Rank	Low Price Rank	RP Rank
RP4					
Texaco, Inc.	TX	+4.96%	3	2	2
Standard Oil, California	SD	-3.96%	4	1	3
American Telephone and Telegraph	T	+26.13%	2		4
American Can	AC	+14.07%	5	5	5
Total Average Return		**+10.30%**			

Total Average Return of S&P 500	**+6.27%**
Total Average Return of Dow 30	**-0.12%**

1985

Company	Tkr	Return	High Yield Rank	Low Price Rank	RP Rank
High-Yield 10					
Union Carbide	UK	+107.16%	*1*	5	2
Texaco, Inc.	TX	-0.74%	*2*	4	1
Chevron	CHV	+31.36%	*3*	3	3
Exxon Corp	XON	+30.22%	*4*		6
General Motors	GM	+0.10%	*5*		16
American Telephone and Telegraph	T	+34.16%	*6*	1	4
Goodyear Tire and Rubber	GT	+26.60%	*7*	2	5
DuPont	DD	+42.31%	*8*		9
American Brands	AMB	+8.86%	*9*		15
American Can	AC	+26.05%	*10*		11
Total Average Return		**+30.61%**			

Company	Tkr	Return	High Yield Rank	Low Price Rank	RP Rank
Foolish Four					
American Telephone and Telegraph	T	+34.16%	6	*1*	4
Goodyear Tire and Rubber	GT	+26.60%	7	*2*	5
Chevron	CHV	+31.36%	3	*3*	3
Texaco, Inc.	TX	-0.74%	2	*4*	1
Total Average Return		**+22.85%**			

Company	Tkr	Return	High Yield Rank	Low Price Rank	RP Rank
RP4					
Union Carbide	UK	+107.16%	1	5	*2*
Chevron	CHV	+31.36%	3	3	*3*
American Telephone and Telegraph	T	+34.16%	6	1	*4*
Goodyear Tire and Rubber	GT	+26.60%	7	2	*5*
Total Average Return		**+49.82%**			

Total Average Return of S&P 500   +32.16%
Total Average Return of Dow 30   +30.98%

1986

Company	Tkr	Return	High Yield Rank	Low Price Rank	RP Rank
High-Yield 10					
Texaco, Inc.	TX	+29.27%	*1*	2	1
General Motors	GM	+1.41%	*2*		8
Exxon Corp	XON	+38.72%	*3*		5
Chevron	CHV	+29.07%	*4*	4	2
Eastman Kodak	EK	+41.26%	*5*		6
Goodyear Tire and Rubber	GT	+43.47%	*6*	3	4
American Telephone and Telegraph	T	+7.41%	*7*	1	3
American Can	AC	+46.82%	*8*		11
International Paper	IP	+57.05%	*9*	5	10
Union Carbide	UK	-0.17%	*10*		14
Total Average Return		**+29.43%**			
Foolish Four					
American Telephone and Telegraph	T	+7.41%	7	*1*	3
Texaco, Inc.	TX	+29.27%	1	*2*	1
Goodyear Tire and Rubber	GT	+43.47%	6	*3*	4
Chevron	CHV	+29.07%	4	*4*	2
Total Average Return		**+27.30%**			
RP4					
Chevron	CHV	+29.07%	4	4	*2*
American Telephone and Telegraph	T	+7.41%	7	1	*3*
Goodyear Tire and Rubber	GT	+43.47%	6	3	*4*
Exxon Corp	XON	+38.72%	3		*5*
Total Average Return		**+29.67%**			

Total Average Return of S&P 500　　+18.47%
Total Average Return of Dow 30　　+21.87%

1987

Company	Tkr	Return	High Yield Rank	Low Price Rank	RP Rank
High-Yield 10					
Texaco, Inc.	TX	+3.40%	*1*	4	2
General Motors	GM	+2.06%	*2*		5
Union Carbide	UK	+5.46%	*3*	2	1
USX, Inc.	X	+49.49%	*4*	1	3
Chevron	CHV	-4.29%	*5*		6
Exxon Corp	XON	+17.78%	*6*		9
American Telephone and Telegraph	T	+16.63%	*7*	3	4
Allied Signal	ALD	-19.57%	*8*	5	7
Sears, Roebuck	S	-8.84%	*9*		8
Philip Morris	MO	+23.50%	*10*		12
Total Average Return		**+8.56%**			

Company	Tkr	Return	High Yield Rank	Low Price Rank	RP Rank
Foolish Four					
USX, Inc.	X	+49.49%	4	*1*	3
Union Carbide	UK	+5.46%	3	*2*	1
American Telephone and Telegraph	T	+16.63%	7	*3*	4
Texaco, Inc.	TX	+3.40%	1	*4*	2
Total Average Return		**+18.75%**			

Company	Tkr	Return	High Yield Rank	Low Price Rank	RP Rank
RP4					
Texaco, Inc.	TX	+3.40%	1	4	*2*
USX, Inc.	X	+49.49%	4	1	*3*
American Telephone and Telegraph	T	+16.63%	7	3	*4*
General Motors	GM	+2.06%	2		*5*
Total Average Return		**+17.89%**			

Total Average Return of S&P 500   +5.23%
Total Average Return of Dow 30   +15.93%

1988

Company	Tkr	Return	High Yield Rank	Low Price Rank	RP Rank
High-Yield 10					
General Motors	GM	+37.94%	*1*		4
Union Carbide	UK	+18.34%	*2*	1	1
Primerica	PRM	+16.65%	*3*	2	2
Allied Signal	ALD	+13.93%	*4*	4	3
Chevron	CHV	+16.04%	*5*		6
Sears, Roebuck	S	+19.79%	*6*		5
Exxon Corp	XON	+12.10%	*7*		8
American Telephone and Telegraph	T	+5.58%	*8*	3	7
Philip Morris	MO	+19.74%	*9*		18
United Technologies	UTX	+19.50%	*10*	5	9
Total Average Return		**+17.96%**			
Foolish Four					
Union Carbide	UK	+18.34%	2	*1*	1
Primerica	PRM	+16.65%	3	*2*	2
American Telephone and Telegraph	T	+5.58%	8	*3*	7
Allied Signal	ALD	+13.93%	4	*4*	3
Total Average Return		**+13.62%**			
RP4					
Primerica	PRM	+16.65%	3	2	*2*
Allied Signal	ALD	+13.93%	4	4	*3*
General Motors	GM	+37.94%	1		*4*
Sears, Roebuck	S	+19.79%	6		*5*
Total Average Return		**+22.08%**			

Total Average Return of S&P 500   +16.81%
Total Average Return of Dow 30   +13.78%

1989

Company	Tkr	Return	High Yield Rank	Low Price Rank	RP Rank
High-Yield 10					
General Motors	GM	+15.50%	1		9
Texaco, Inc.	TX	+37.69%	2		4
Chevron	CHV	+57.21%	3		3
Allied Signal	ALD	+11.39%	4	2	1
Exxon Corp	XON	+20.92%	5	4	7
Sears, Roebuck	S	+0.93%	6	3	6
USX, Inc.	X	+27.86%	7	1	2
Eastman Kodak	EK	+0.56%	8	5	8
Philip Morris	MO	+74.47%	9		18
DuPont	DD	+49.90%	10		16
Total Average Return		**+29.64%**			

Company	Tkr	Return	High Yield Rank	Low Price Rank	RP Rank
Foolish Four					
USX, Inc.	X	+27.86%	7	1	2
Allied Signal	ALD	+11.39%	4	2	1
Sears, Roebuck	S	+0.93%	6	3	6
Exxon Corp	XON	+20.92%	5	4	7
Total Average Return		**+15.28%**			

Company	Tkr	Return	High Yield Rank	Low Price Rank	RP Rank
RP4					
USX, Inc.	X	+27.86%	7	1	2
Chevron	CHV	+57.21%	3		3
Texaco, Inc.	TX	+37.69%	2		4
American Telephone and Telegraph	T	+66.64%			5
Total Average Return		**+47.35%**			

Total Average Return of S&P 500	**+31.49%**	
Total Average Return of Dow 30	**+31.95%**	

1990

Company	Tkr	Return	High Yield Rank	Low Price Rank	RP Rank
High-Yield 10					
General Motors	GM	-16.29%	*1*	5	1
Sears, Roebuck	S	-28.06%	*2*	3	4
Allied Signal	ALD	-15.76%	*3*	2	2
Texaco, Inc.	TX	+6.00%	*4*		7
International Business Machines	IBM	+19.35%	*5*		10
Exxon Corp	XON	+6.44%	*6*		6
Eastman Kodak	EK1	+0.58%	*4*	5	
Union Carbide	UK	-27.18%	*8*	1	3
Chevron	CHV	+8.97%	*9*		13
Goodyear Tire and Rubber	GT	-54.16%	*10*		9
Total Average Return		**-10.01%**			
Foolish Four					
Union Carbide	UK	-27.18%	8	*1*	3
Allied Signal	ALD	-15.76%	3	*2*	2
Sears, Roebuck	S	-28.06%	2	*3*	4
Eastman Kodak	EK	+0.58%	7	*4*	5
Total Average Return		**-17.61%**			
RP4					
Allied Signal	ALD	-15.76%	3	2	*2*
Union Carbide	UK	-27.18%	8	1	*3*
Sears, Roebuck	S	-28.06%	2	3	*4*
Eastman Kodak	EK	+0.58%	7	4	*5*
Total Average Return		**-17.61%**			

Total Average Return of S&P 500   -3.17%
Total Average Return of Dow 30   -9.14%

1991

Company	Tkr	Return	High Yield Rank	Low Price Rank	RP Rank
High-Yield 10					
Goodyear Tire and Rubber	GT	+182.37%	*1*	2	1
General Motors	GM	-4.82%	*2*		3
Sears, Roebuck	S	+57.00%	*3*	3	2
Allied Signal	ALD	+55.71%	*4*	4	5
Union Carbide	UK	+31.34%	*5*	1	4
Texaco, Inc.	TX	+8.30%	*6*		14
Exxon Corp	XON	+23.51%	*7*		13
Westinghouse Electric	WX	-30.75%	*8*	5	7
Eastman Kodak	EK	+24.62%	*9*		12
USX, Inc.	X	+5.13%	*10*		8
Total Average Return		**+35.24%**			
Foolish Four					
Union Carbide	UK	+31.34%	5	*1*	4
Goodyear Tire and Rubber	GT	+182.37%	1	*2*	1
Sears, Roebuck	S	+57.00%	3	*3*	2
Allied Signal	ALD	+55.71%	4	*4*	5
Total Average Return		**+81.61%**			
RP4					
Sears, Roebuck	S	+57.00%	3	3	*2*
General Motors	GM	-4.82%	2		*3*
Union Carbide	UK	+31.34%	5	1	*4*
Allied Signal	ALD	+55.71%	4	4	*5*
Total Average Return		**+34.81%**			
Total Average Return of S&P 500		**+30.55%**			
Total Average Return of Dow 30		**+30.36%**			

1992

Company	Tkr	Return	High Yield Rank	Low Price Rank	RP Rank
High-Yield 10					
Westinghouse Electric	WX	-20.03%	*1*	1	1
International Business Machines	IBM	-39.10%	*2*		12
Texaco, Inc.	TX	+2.77%	*3*		8
Sears, Roebuck	S	+22.01%	*4*	5	5
General Motors	GM	+10.56%	*5*	4	4
American Express	AXP	+24.10%	*6*	2	2
Chevron	CHV	+6.06%	*7*		10
Union Carbide	UK	+63.10%	*8*	3	3
Exxon Corp	XON	+7.01%	*9*		11
Eastman Kodak	EK	-12.94%	*10*		9
Total Average Return		**+6.35%**			
Foolish Four					
American Express	AXP	+24.10%	6	*2*	2
Union Carbide	UK	+63.10%	8	*3*	3
General Motors	GM	+10.56%	5	*4*	4
Sears, Roebuck	S	+22.01%	4	*5*	5
Total Average Return		**+29.94%**			
RP4					
American Express	AXP	+24.10%	6	2	*2*
Union Carbide	UK	+63.10%	8	3	*3*
General Motors	GM	+10.56%	5	4	*4*
Sears, Roebuck	S	+22.01%	4	5	*5*
Total Average Return		**+29.94%**			

Total Average Return of S&P 500   +7.67%
Total Average Return of Dow 30   +11.00%

1993

Company	Tkr	Return	High Yield Rank	Low Price Rank	RP Rank
High-Yield 10					
International Business Machines	IBM	+18.11%	*1*		2
Texaco, Inc.	TX	+14.74%	*2*		6
Westinghouse Electric	WX	+1.98%	*3*	1	1
Eastman Kodak	EK	+41.90%	*4*	4	5
Chevron	CHV	+31.18%	*5*		10
Exxon Corp	XON	+8.56%	*6*		9
Union Carbide	UK	+38.52%	*7*	2	3
Sears, Roebuck	S	+47.57%	*8*	5	7
American Express	AXP	+22.50%	*9*	3	4
Morgan, J.P.	JPM	+10.33%	*10*		13
Total Average Return		**+23.54%**			
Foolish Four					
Westinghouse Electric	WX	+1.98%	3	*1*	1
Union Carbide	UK	+38.52%	7	*2*	3
American Express	AXP	+22.50%	9	*3*	4
Eastman Kodak	EK	+41.90%	4	*4*	5
Total Average Return		**+26.22%**			
RP4					
International Business Machines	IBM	+18.11%	1		*2*
Union Carbide	UK	+38.52%	7	2	*3*
American Express	AXP	+22.50%	9	3	*4*
Eastman Kodak	EK	+41.90%	4	4	*5*
Total Average Return		**+30.26%**			

Total Average Return of S&P 500   +9.99%
Total Average Return of Dow 30   +17.91%

1994

Company	Tkr	Return	High Yield Rank	Low Price Rank	RP Rank
High-Yield 10					
Texaco, Inc.	TX	-2.75%	1		5
Exxon Corp	XON	-0.34%	2		7
Philip Morris	MO	+5.26%	3		6
Woolworth	Z	-37.78%	4	2	1
Chevron	CHV	+5.34%	5		13
Morgan, J.P.	JPM	-14.54%	6		11
Eastman Kodak	EK	+12.44%	7	5	10
DuPont	DD	+16.81%	8	4	9
American Express	AXP	+12.78%	9	3	4
Union Carbide	UK	+27.07%	10	1	3
Total Average Return		**+2.43%**			
Foolish Four					
Union Carbide	UK	+27.07%	10	1	3
Woolworth	Z	-37.78%	4	2	1
American Express	AXP	+12.78%	9	3	4
DuPont	DD	+16.81%	8	4	9
Total Average Return		**+4.72%**			
RP4					
Westinghouse Electric	WX	-6.73%			2
Union Carbide	UK	+27.07%	10	1	3
American Express	AXP	+12.78%	9	3	4
Texaco, Inc.	TX	-2.75%	1		5
Total Average Return		**+7.59%**			

Total Average Return of S&P 500   +1.31%
Total Average Return of Dow 30   +3.73%

1995

Company	Tkr	Return	High Yield Rank	Low Price Rank	RP Rank
High-Yield 10					
Philip Morris	MO	+65.79%	*1*		2
Morgan, J.P.	JPM	+49.00%	*2*		3
Texaco, Inc.	TX	+35.45%	*3*		4
Exxon Corp	XON	+37.94%	*4*		5
Chevron	CHV	+23.15%	*5*	2	6
Woolworth	Z	-13.66%	*6*	1	1
Sears, Roebuck	S	+67.03%	*7*	3	10
du Pont	DD	+32.20%	*8*		13
Eastman Kodak	EK	+45.17%	*9*	4	11
Minnesota, Mining and Manufacturing	MMM	+28.94%	*10*	5	15
Total Average Return		**+37.10%**			
Foolish Four					
Woolworth	Z	-13.66%	6	*1*	1
Chevron	CHV	+23.15%	5	*2*	6
Sears, Roebuck	S	+67.03%	7	*3*	10
Eastman Kodak	EK	+45.17%	9	*4*	11
Total Average Return		**30.42%**			
RP4					
Philip Morris	MO	+65.79%	1		*2*
Morgan, J.P.	JPM	+49.00%	2		*3*
Texaco, Inc.	TX	+35.45%	3		*4*
Exxon Corp	XON	+37.94%	4		*5*
Total Average Return		**+47.05%**			

Total Average Return of S&P 500	**+37.43%**
Total Average Return of Dow 30	**+36.69%**

1996

Company	Tkr	Return	High Yield Rank	Low Price Rank	RP Rank
High-Yield 10					
Philip Morris	MO	+26.15%	1		3
Texaco, Inc.	TX	+30.70%	2		2
Morgan, J.P.	JPM	+23.49%	3		4
Chevron	CHV	+28.52%	4	2	1
Exxon Corp	XON	+25.89%	5		5
DuPont	DD	+35.74%	6	5	8
Minnesota Mining and Manufacturing	MMM	+34.37%	7	4	9
International Paper	IP	+9.27%	8	1	6
General Electric	GE	+35.41%	9		15
Caterpillar	CAT	+25.21%	10	3	14
Total Average Return		**+27.47%**			
Foolish Four					
International Paper	IP	+9.27%	8	1	
Chevron	CHV	+28.52%	4	2	
Caterpillar	CAT	+25.21%	10	3	
Minnesota Mining and Manufacturing	MMM	+34.37%	7	4	
Total Average Return		**+24.34%**			
RP					
Texaco, Inc.	TX	+30.70%	2		2
Philip Morris	MO	+26.15%	1		3
Morgan, J.P.	JPM	+23.49%	3		4
Exxon Corp	XON	+25.89%	5		5
Total Average Return		**+26.56%**			

Total Average Return of S&P 500   +23.07%
Total Average Return of Dow 30   +24.32%

1997

Company	Tkr	Return	High Yield Rank	Low Price Rank	RP Rank
High-Yield Ten					
Philip Morris	MO	+26.22%	*1*		2
Morgan, J.P.	JPM	+19.32%	*2*		5
Texaco, Inc.	TX	+10.92%	*3*		7
Chevron	CHV	+21.77%	*4*	4	3
Exxon Corp	XON	+29.10%	*5*		8
AT&T	T	+43.60%	*6*	2	1
General Motors	GM	+13.24%	*7*	3	6
International Paper	IP	+10.63%	*8*	1	4
DuPont	DD	+29.80%	*9*		14
Minnesota Mining and Manufacturing	MMM	-0.73%	*10*	5	13
Total Average Return		**+20.39%**			
Foolish Four					
International Paper	IP	+10.63%	8	*1*	4
AT&T	T	+43.60%	6	*2*	1
General Motors	GM	+13.24%	7	*3*	6
Chevron	CHV	+21.77%	4	*4*	3
Total Average Return		**+22.31%**			
RP					
Philip Morris	MO	+26.22%	1		*2*
Chevron	CHV	+21.77%	4	4	*3*
International Paper	IP	+10.63%	8	1	*4*
Morgan, J.P.	JPM	+19.32%	2		*5*
Total Average Return		**+19.49%**			

Total Average Return of S&P 500   +33.36%
Total Average Return of Dow 30   +22.33%

Appendix
D

EFFECTS OF
CAPITAL GAINS
TAXES ON RETURNS

EFFECTS OF CAPITAL GAINS TAXES ON RETURNS

Tax-free or Tax-deferred
Retirement Account vs. Taxable Account

	Retirement Account: Foolish Four @21.86%*	Taxable Account: Foolish Four @21.86%*	Taxes paid: 20% on annual gain
Starting Amount and Annual Contribution	$2,000.00	$2,000.00	
End of Year 1	$4,327.20	$4,327.20	$74.88
Year 2	$7,163.13	$7,071.88	$162.01
Year 3	$10,618.99	$10,310.36	$264.77
Year 4	$14,830.30	$14,131.56	$386.02
Year 5	$19,962.20	$18,640.31	$529.09
Year 6	$26,215.93	$23,960.34	$697.89
Year 7	$33,836.74	$30,237.62	$897.08
Year 8	$43,123.45	$37,644.39	$1,132.10
Year 9	$54,440.23	$46,383.88	$1,409.41
Year 10	$68,230.87	$56,695.89	$1,736.61
Year 11	$85,036.14	$68,863.38	$2,122.69
Year 12	$105,515.04	$83,220.20	$2,578.24
Year 13	$130,470.62	$100,160.29	$3,115.76
Year 14	$160,881.50	$120,148.45	$3,750.00
Year 15	$197,940.20	$143,733.16	$4,498.36
Year 16	$243,099.93	$171,561.52	$5,381.37
Year 17	$298,131.57	$204,397.14	$6,423.26
Year 18	$365,193.13	$243,140.96	$7,652.63
Year 19	$446,914.35	$288,856.08	$9,103.20
Year 20	$546,499.83	$342,796.87	$10,814.77
Year 21	$667,854.69	$406,443.38	$12,834.31
Year 22	$815,737.73	$481,542.01	$15,217.24
Year 23	$995,948.00	$570,153.36	$18,028.93
Year 24	$1,215,552.23	$674,708.83	$21,346.54
Year 25	$1,483,161.95	$798,077.28	$25,261.10
Total Taxes paid	$0.00		$155,418.27
Account Value	$1,483,161.95	$798,077.28	

*Actual 25-Year Average Annual Return (CAGR) 1963–1997
Note: $110 deducted annually for commissions and fees for both accounts

A retirement account has a strong advantage over accounts that are subject to capital gains taxes. However, in the example above, no additional taxes would be due on money withdrawn from the non-retirement account. Withdrawals from the retirement account would be subject to regular earned income taxes if the account were a 401(k), Keogh, SEP-IRA, or traditional IRA. If it were a Roth IRA, the money could be withdrawn tax-free after age 59 1/2.

Effects of Capital Gains Taxes on Returns

The Foolish Four Compared with a Low Turnover S&P 500 Index Fund

	Foolish Four @21.86%*	Taxes paid: 20% on annual gain	S&P Index Fund @13.06%*	Taxes paid on 1% turnover
Starting Amount and Annual Contribution	$2,000.00		$2,000.00	
End of Year 1	$4,264.40	$52.88	$4,261.20	$8.52
Year 2	$6,889.92	$125.10	$6,808.08	$13.62
Year 3	$9,921.19	$206.25	$9,681.82	$19.36
Year 4	$13,423.57	$300.48	$12,924.37	$25.85
Year 5	$17,469.73	$409.23	$16,583.07	$33.17
Year 6	$22,144.23	$534.90	$20,711.32	$41.42
Year 7	$27,544.59	$680.07	$25,369.39	$50.74
Year 8	$33,783.56	$847.79	$30,625.26	$61.25
Year 9	$40,991.34	$1,041.56	$36,555.67	$73.11
Year 10	$49,318.38	$1,265.41	$43,247.18	$86.49
Year 11	$58,938.49	$1,524.02	$50,797.47	$101.59
Year 12	$70,052.46	$1,822.79	$59,316.76	$118.63
Year 13	$82,892.26	$2,167.96	$68,929.40	$137.86
Year 14	$97,725.89	$2,566.73	$79,775.72	$159.55
Year 15	$114,862.96	$3,027.41	$92,014.04	$184.03
Year 16	$134,661.16	$3,559.64	$105,823.01	$211.65
Year 17	$157,533.72	$4,174.51	$121,404.21	$242.81
Year 18	$183,958.06	$4,884.87	$138,985.08	$277.97
Year 19	$214,485.69	$5,705.53	$158,822.26	$317.64
Year 20	$249,753.81	$6,653.62	$181,205.32	$362.41
Year 21	$290,498.54	$7,748.95	$206,460.99	$412.92
Year 22	$337,570.32	$9,014.36	$234,957.95	$469.92
Year 23	$391,951.64	$10,476.26	$267,112.17	$534.22
Year 24	$454,777.57	$12,165.19	$303,393.02	$606.79
Year 25	$527,359.42	$14,116.37	$344,330.12	$688.66
Account liquidated				
Taxes paid through Year 25	$95,071.88		$5,240.19	
Additional taxes due	$0		$67,417.99	
Total Taxes Paid	**$95,071.88**		**$72,658.18**	
Account Value	**$527,359.42**		**$276,912.13**	

*For this example we are using the lower 35-Year Average Annual Return (CAGR 1963–1997) for the Foolish Four. We used the higher 25-year return for the S&P. Yep, that handicaps the Foolish Four, but we like to be conservative. For Foolish Four returns using the 25-year CAGR, see the previous page.

Note 1: Very few mutual funds have performed as well as the S&P Index fund over a long time period.

Note 2: We subtracted $110 per year for commissions and fees from the Foolish Four account but not the Index fund account. (It can't afford them!)

Appendix
E

RESOURCES

RESOURCES
(online areas, books, etc.)

The Motley Fool Website

The Motley Fool home page address:
http://www.fool.com

The Dow Dividend Approach:
http://www.fool.com/links/dowinvesting.htm

Detailed Stock Quotations:
http://quote.fool.com/detailed.asp

Current Dow Approach Selections (updated each trading day):
http://www.fool.com/links/currentdoworder.htm

Motley Fool Tax Area:
http://www.fool.com/school/taxes/taxes.htm

Motley Fool Message Boards:
http://boards.fool.com/Folders.asp

(Note: Folders on individual companies are in "Stocks A to Z" and the Dow Dividend Approach folder is in "Investors' Roundtable." You must register to post new messages on our boards. Registration is free. You may read any message without registering.)

FoolMart:
http://www.foolmart.com

Other Web Resources

Dow Jones Averages Homepage:
http://averages.dowjones.com/home.html

Dow Jones Industrial Average Companies
   & Links to Webpages:
http://averages.dowjones.com/djia_cos.html

Dow Data:
http://averages.dowjones.com/dowdata.html

Dow Jones Industrial Average History:
http://averages.dowjones.com/abtdjia.html

About Charles Dow:
http://averages.dowjones.com/chDow.html

Amex DIAMONDS (Index Shares on the Dow Jones
   Industrial Average):
http://www.amex.com/diamonds/info/index.html

The Wall Street Journal Annual Reports Service (free):
http://www.icbinc.com/cgi-bin/wsj.pl

Tax Information from the IRS:
http://www.irs.ustreas.gov/

Financial Data Finder
(Ohio State University, Fisher College of Business):
http://www.cob.ohio-state.edu/dept/fin/osudata.htm

S&P Stock Index Information:
http://www.advisorinsight.com/pub/indexes

Some Books of Interest

The Motley Fool Investment Guide,
by David and Tom Gardner

The Motley Fool Investment Workbook,
by David and Tom Gardner

You Have More Than You Think,
by David and Tom Gardner

The Unemotional Investor,
by Robert Sheard

Built to Last: Successful Habits of Visionary Companies,
by James C. Collins & Jerry I. Porras

Beating the Dow,
Michael O'Higgins

The Dividend Investor,
Knowles & Petty

What Works on Wall Street,
James P. O'Shaughnessy

Stock Market Logic,
Norman Fosback

OTHER NEW OFFERINGS FROM THE MOTLEY FOOL

IN BOOKSTORES NOW

To find out about other Motley Fool products, visit us online at www.FoolMart.com (AOL keyword: FoolMart) or call 1-888-665-FOOL for more information

or

send in the order form below to receive your free Motley Fool Catalog.